FLANNERY
SHC

NOTES

including
- *Life of the Author*
- *O'Connor's View of Her Writing*
- *Critical Commentaries*
  A Good Man Is Hard to Find
  The Life You Save May Be Your Own
  The Displaced Person
  The Artificial Nigger
  Good Country People
  Everything That Rises Must Converge
  and Others
- *Some Concluding Considerations*
- *Suggested Essay Questions*
- *Selected Bibliography*

by
Terry J. Dibble, Ph.D.
Professor of English
Milligan College
   at Milligan College, Tennessee

INCORPORATED
LINCOLN, NEBRASKA   68501

Editor

Gary Carey, M.A,
University of Colorado

Consulting Editor

James L. Roberts, Ph.D.
Department of English
University of Nebraska

ISBN 0-8220-0906-4
© Copyright 1986
by
C. K. Hillegass
All Rights Reserved
Printed in U.S.A.

1989 Printing

Cliffs Notes, Inc.   Lincoln, Nebraska

CONTENTS

FLANNERY O'CONNOR'S SHORT STORIES
Notes

LIFE OF THE AUTHOR

Mary Flannery O'Connor, the only child of Edward Francis O'Connor and Regina Cline O'Connor, was born in Savannah, Georgia, on March 25, 1925. When she was five years old, a Pathé newsreel featured her and a pet Bantam chicken possessed of the ability to walk both backward and forward. Some critics have suggested that this chicken was early evidence of her later interest in the grotesque which is so much a part of her fiction. Be that or not, it is evidence of her abiding passion for fowl, a passion later gratified by the multitude of ducks, geese, guineas, peafowl, and other assorted birds with which she was to populate her mother's dairy farm, Andalusia.

O'Connor attended St. Vincent's, a Catholic parochial school in Savannah, until 1938, when the family, as a result of her father's illness, moved to Milledgeville. There they took up residence in her mother's ancestral home, an antebellum brick house which had been constructed in the 1820s. It had served as a temporary governor's mansion when Milledgeville was the capital of Georgia, it had housed General Sherman when he marched through Milledgeville in November of 1864, and it had been purchased by the Cline family in 1886. In addition, it was the very house from which her maternal grandfather, Peter Cline, had served as mayor of Milledgeville for over twenty years.

It was this house and the sense of tradition which it evoked that led O'Connor to describe the parade of visitors through the house during the annual garden club pilgrimage of homes as ". . . the public which trouped through in respectful solemnity to view the past. This was the past which happened to be in excellent working order and in which I lived." It was there that her father died in 1941 from the effects of lupus erythematosus, an incurable disease of metabolic origin which was later to claim O'Connor herself on August 3, 1964.

Since Milledgeville contained only a small Catholic population, one Catholic church and no parochial schools, Flannery attended Peabody High School, from which she graduated in 1942. She then enrolled in the Georgia State College for Women, now known as Georgia College, from which she graduated with a B.A. in social science in 1945. While there she served as editor of the literary quarterly, *The Corinthian*, and as art editor for *The Colonnade*, the student newspaper. The O'Connor collection in the Ina Dillard Russel Library at Georgia College contains a number of cartoons which Flannery produced during these years, showing that even as an undergraduate, she had cultivated an interest in art and was possessed of that wry sense of humor so characteristic of her writing style.

Following graduation, she received a scholarship from and enrolled in the Writers Workshop at the State University of Iowa, receiving a Master of Fine Arts degree from that institution in 1947. On the strength of having her first story, "The Geranium," published in *Accent* magazine in 1946 and having won the Rinehart-Iowa Fiction Award in 1947, O'Connor was recommended for a place at Yaddo, a writers colony located in Saratoga Springs, New York. She remained there only a few months, however, leaving along with all the other writers in residence because of an FBI investigation into the long-term stay of a well-known journalist alleged to be a Communist party member and the negative publicity which was generated because of that investigation.

O'Connor enjoyed the routine at Yaddo, but she would not compromise her conscience. In a letter written to John Shelby, her personal contact at Rinehart, she says, "I am amenable to criticism but only within the sphere of what I am trying to do. I will not be persuaded to do otherwise." It was during this period that O'Connor first met Robert and Sally Fitzgerald, who were to become lifelong friends and, following her death, O'Connor's literary executors.

It was to the Fitzgerald home in Connecticut that O'Connor was to go as a paying guest on September 1, 1949, following a brief stay in Milledgeville, and it was there that she was to spend the majority of her time until December of 1950 when, on her way home for the Christmas holidays, she became severely ill. Admitted to a hospital in Atlanta, her illness was diagnosed as lupus, and the doctors offered her mother little hope that Flannery would recover. Blood transfusions and massive doses of ACTH, at that time an experimental drug, produced a remission of the disease. Following her release from the hospital in 1959, she moved to Andalusia, a dairy farm which her mother had inherited from a brother and which was located near Milledgeville.

Aside from occasional lecture trips to colleges and universities, an occasional trip to visit friends, a trip to Lourdes and an audience with the Pope in 1958, and trips to Notre Dame in 1962 and to Smith College in 1963 to receive honorary Doctor of Letters degrees, O'Connor spent most of the remainder of her life in and around Milledgeville. Her mobility was greatly reduced by the ravages of her disease and/or by the high doses of ACTH which she took to hold the disease in check until finally she was forced to move about on crutches.

Watched over by her mother, O'Connor usually spent the morning hours at her writing while her afternoons were occupied by painting, reading, tending her flocks of peacocks, geese, and chickens, and carrying on a voluminous correspondence with friends and increasingly large numbers of individuals who wrote her concerning her stories.

A large selection of O'Connor's letters, collected and edited by Sally Fitzgerald, reveals much about O'Connor's work habits, possible sources of inspiration for her stories, her concern for her fellow human beings, and her sense of humor. It is here, for example, that one learns that Mrs. Shortley's concern with the Guizac's foreignness in "The Displaced Person" has its origins in a question asked by the wife of Mrs. O'Connor's hired dairyman on the occasion of the arrival of a refugee family to work on the O'Connor farm—"Do you think they'll know what colors even is?"

Numerous other letters also recount the trials of the black couple employed on the farm, as well as reveal O'Connor's rather off-beat sense of humor. To a friend, she writes about the burro that she gave her mother, along with the note, "For the woman who has everything." At another time, O'Connor recounts her response to the little old lady who had written to complain that one of O'Connor's stories was not to her taste; O'Connor replied, "You weren't supposed to eat it."

In February 1964, O'Connor underwent surgery for a benign tumor, and this surgery reactivated the lupus from which she died on August 3, 1964.

O'CONNOR'S VIEW OF HER WRITING

O'Connor appears to have developed, at a very early stage in her writing career, a sense of direction and purpose which allowed her to reject vigorously even proposed revisions suggested by Mr. Shelby, her contact at Rinehart. If changes were called for, she herself wanted to make them, and she did. In fact, the experimentation with atmosphere and tone which characterized the five stories in her master's thesis at Iowa and the seeming uncertainty about the direction of her work, which she expressed in an early letter to Elizabeth McKee, her literary agent, was replaced in less than a year by such a degree of self-confidence that she became interested in finding another publishing company for her yet-to-be-completed first novel.

In July 1948, O'Connor had written to McKee, "I don't have my novel outlined and I have to write to discover what I am doing. Like the old lady, I don't know so well what I think until I see what I say; then I have to say it over again." In February 1949, she wrote to McKee again, "I want mainly to be where they will take the book as I write it." Two weeks later, she wrote again to McKee, concerning a letter received from Shelby, "I presume Shelby says either that Rinehart will not take the novel as it will be if left to my fiendish care (it will be essentially as it is), or that Rinehart would like to rescue it at this point and train it into a conventional novel. . . . The letter [Shelby's letter to O'Connor] is addressed to a slightly dim-witted Camp Fire Girl, and I cannot look with composure on getting a lifetime of others like them."

The following day, O'Connor wrote to Mr. Shelby, "I feel that whatever virtues the novel may have are very much connected with the limitations you mention. I am not writing a conventional novel, and I think that the quality of the novel I write will derive precisely from the peculiarity or aloneness, if you will, of the experience I wrote from."

We may never know, as some critics suggest, whether O'Connor found in the writings of Nathaniel West, another American writer, confirmation of ". . . the odd comic look of her world," or whether this confirmation strengthened her self-confidence to the extent that she could reject Shelby's suggested revisions. There is, however, evidence of O'Connor's acquaintance with West's work — especially in her story "The Peeler," a short story which first appeared in the December 1949 *Partisan Review,* and which was later revised to become Chapter 3 of *Wise Blood.*

West's cynical Willie Shrike, Miss Lonelyhearts' editor (from West's *Miss Lonelyhearts*), appears reborn in Asa Shrike, the blind street preacher in "The Peeler"; he is then further transformed into Asa Hawks, the supposedly blind street preacher who cynically uses his "blindness," as well as his feigned religion, to wheedle a meager living from the people of Taulkingham (O'Connor's equivalent of Atlanta). When Hazel Motes (the protagonist of *Wise Blood*) discovers Hawks' fraud, the revelation functions as one of the turning points which leads Hazel to reevaluate his life and to turn again to the religion from which he had so desperately attempted to flee. Although one may grant West's influence on the overall tone and the style of O'Connor's writing, one must remember that, as one critic has suggested, "West and O'Connor wrote out of opposing religious commitments."

With the exception of a number of the early stories, O'Connor consistently produced fiction having an implicit, if not a totally explicit, religious world view as an integral element of each work. This should come as no surprise to anyone familiar with her habit of attending mass each morning while she was at Iowa and going to mass with one of the Fitzgeralds each morning while she was in Connecticut. Even though O'Connor was, according to all available evidence, a devout Catholic, she did not let her religious conservatism interfere with the practice of her craft.

In numerous articles and letters to her friends, O'Connor stressed the need for the Catholic writer to make fiction "according to its nature . . . by grounding it in concrete observable reality" because when the Catholic writer "closes his own eyes and tries to see with the eyes of the Church, the result is another addition to that large body of pious trash for which we have so long been famous." As she noted in one article, "When people have told me that because I am a Catholic, I cannot be an artist, I have had to reply, ruefully, that because I am a Catholic, I cannot afford to be less than an artist."

O'Connor's concern with the generally low quality of religious literature and the typical lack of literary acumen among the average readers of religious stories led her to expend large amounts of her carefully managed energy in order to produce book reviews for *The Bulletin,* a diocesan paper of limited circulation, because, as she wrote a friend, it was ". . . the only corporal work of mercy open to me."

This, in spite of the fact that she had written to the same friend concerning her frustrations with the inaccurate reporting by *The Bulletin* of some of her comments: "They didn't want to hear what I said and when they heard it they didn't want to believe it and so they changed it. I also told them that the average Catholic reader was a Militant Moron but they didn't quote that naturally."

As a writer with professedly Christian concerns, O'Connor was, throughout her writing career, convinced that the majority of her audience did not share her basic viewpoint and was, if not openly hostile to it, at best indifferent. In order to reach such an audience, O'Connor felt that she had to make the basic distortions of a world separated from the original, divine plan ". . . appear as distortions to an audience which is used to seeing them as natural." This she accomplished by resorting to the grotesque in her fiction.

To the "true believer," the "ultimate grotesqueness" is found in those postlapsarian (after the Fall) individuals who ignore their proper relationship to the Divine and either rebel against It or deny that they have any need to rely upon It for help in this life. In the first category, one would find those characters like Hazel Motes or Francis Marion Tarwater (the protagonists of her two novels), who flee from the call of the Divine only to find themselves pursued by It and ultimately forced to accept their role as children of God. Likewise, the Misfit, having finally decided to reject the account of Christ having raised Lazarus from the dead because he had not been there to witness it, accepts this world and its temporal pleasures only to discover, "It's no real pleasure in life."

In the second category, one can find those prideful, self-reliant individuals such as the Misfit and the grandmother (from "A Good Man Is Hard to Find"), Mrs. McIntyre (from "The Displaced Person"), and Hulga Hopewell (from "Good Country People"), who feel that they have conquered life because they are especially pious, prudent, and hardworking. To make these individuals appear grotesque to the secular humanist (one who argues that man can, by his own ingenuity and wisdom, make a paradise of this earth, if given sufficient time), O'Connor creates, for example, (1) the psychopathic killer, (2) the pious fraud, or (3) the physical or intellectual cripple. This display of what some critics have labeled the "gratuitous grotesque" became for O'Connor the means by which she hoped to capture the attention of her audience. She wrote in a very early essay, "When you can assume that your audience holds the same beliefs you do, you can relax a little and use more normal means of talking to it; when you have to assume that it does not, then you have to make your vision apparent by shock – to the hard of hearing you shout, and for the almost-blind you draw large and startling figures." For O'Connor, writing was a long, continuous shout.

No examination of O'Connor's view of her fiction would be complete without mentioning a couple of comments that she made concerning the nature of her work; in fact, anyone particularly interested in O'Connor should read *Mystery and Manners,* a collection of O'Connor's occasional prose, selected and edited by the Fitzgeralds. At one point in a section of that book entitled "On Her Own Work," O'Connor notes, "There is a moment in every great story in which the presence of grace can be felt as it waits to be accepted or rejected, even though the reader may not recognize this moment."

At another point, she comments, "From my own experience in trying to make stories 'work,' I have discovered that what is needed is an action that is totally unexpected, yet totally believable, and I have found that, for me, this is always an action which indicates that grace has been offered. And frequently it is an action in which the devil has been the unwilling instrument of grace."

Without becoming totally bogged down in the Catholic doctrine of grace (a good Catholic dictionary will list at least ten to fifteen entries dealing with the subject), one should be aware of what O'Connor means when she uses the term in connection with her stories. Loosely defined, Illuminating Grace (the type of grace most frequently used by O'Connor in her stories) may be described as a gift, freely given by God, which is designed to enlighten the minds of men and help them toward eternal life. It may take the form of some natural mental experience, such as a dream or viewing a beautiful sunset, or of some experience imposed from outside the individual – for example, from hearing a sermon or from experiencing an intense joy, a sorrow, or some other shock.

Man, having been given free will, may, according to the Catholic position, elect not to accept the gift of grace, as opposed to a Calvinist position, which argues for a concept of Irresistible Grace – that is, man cannot reject God's grace when it is given to him. Even though O'Connor notes that she looks for the moment ". . . in which the presence of grace can be felt as it waits to be accepted or rejected," one should not assume that she is attempting to pass judgment on the ultimate fate of her characters. That, from an orthodox point of view, is not possible for man to do. It is for this reason (much to the bewilderment of some of her readers) that O'Connor can say of the Misfit, "I prefer to think, however unlikely this may seem, the old lady's gesture . . . will be enough of a pain to him there to turn him into the prophet he was meant to become."

Even though O'Connor's vision was essentially religious, she chose to present it from a primarily comic or grotesque perspective. In a note to the second edition of *Wise Blood,* her first novel, O'Connor wrote, "It is a comic novel about a Christian *malgré lui* [in spite of himself], and as such, very serious, for all comic novels that are any good must be about matters of life and death." Several friends have verified O'Connor's problem with public readings of her stories.

When on lecture tours, O'Connor habitually read "A Good Man Is Hard to Find" because it was one of the few of her stories which she could read without breaking out in laughter. One acquaintance who had taken a class of students to Andalusia in order to meet O'Connor and to listen to a reading of one of her stories reported that as O'Connor neared the end of "Good Country People," ". . . her reading had to be interrupted for perhaps as much as a minute while she laughed. I really doubted whether she would be able to finish the story."

For individuals incapable of seeing humanity as a group of struggling manikins operating against a backdrop of eternal purpose, many of O'Connor's stories appear to be filled with meaningless violence. Even those characters who are granted a moment of grace or experience an epiphanal vision do so only at the cost of having their self-images, if not themselves, destroyed. In a very real sense, all of O'Connor's characters have inherited the Original Sin of Adam and all are equally guilty. The only distinction to be made between them is that some come to an awareness of their situation and some do not.

A GOOD MAN IS HARD TO FIND

First published in 1953, following her permanent move to Andalusia, her mother's dairy farm, "A Good Man Is Hard to Find" illustrates many of the techniques and themes which were to characterize the typical O'Connor story. Since she was limited by her illness to short and infrequent trips away from the farm, O'Connor learned to draw upon the resources at hand for the subject matter of her stories. These resources included the people around her, her reading material, which consisted of various books and periodicals which came to Andalusia, and an assortment of local and regional newspapers. Several critics have pointed out the influence of regional and local newspaper stories on O'Connor's fiction. The Misfit, the pathological killer who murders an entire family in this story, was apparently fabricated from newspaper accounts of two criminals who had terrorized the Atlanta area in the early '50s; Red Sammy Butts, according to another critic, may have been based on a local "good ole boy" who had made good and returned to Milledgeville each year, on the occasion of his birthday, to attend a banquet in his honor, hosted by the local merchants.

O'Connor's treatment of the characters in this story reinforces her view of man as a fallen creature. Briefly, the story depicts the destruction of an altogether too normal family by three escaped convicts. The thematic climax of the story involves an offer of grace and the grandmother's acceptance of that gift as a result of the epiphany she experiences just before her death. The events which lead to that climax, however, generate much of the interest of the story.

The reader's first view of the family is one designed to illustrate the disrespect and dissension which characterize the family's relationships with one another. The grandmother's vanity and self-centered attitude are made apparent in the first three lines of the story. Rather than acquiesce to the family's plan for a trip to Florida, she wishes to visit some of her "connections" in east Tennessee. In the next line, one learns that Bailey is her only son, a bit of information which prevents a possible misreading of the grandmother's last earthly words, "You're one of my children," and thereby prevents the reader from missing the action of grace at the end of the story. In her attempt to get the family to go to Tennessee rather than to Florida, the grandmother uses the news story of the escaped murderer, the Misfit, to try to scare Bailey into changing his mind. Although Bailey does not answer her (thereby showing a complete lack of respect for her), the incident provides an ironic foreshadowing to the end of the story.

When Bailey fails to respond to her pressure, the grandmother attempts to get her daughter-in-law, a dull young woman with a face "as broad and innocent as a cabbage," to help her convince Bailey to go to Tennessee rather than Florida because the children, John Wesley and June Star, have not yet visited Tennessee. Bailey's wife also ignores the plea, but the non-vocal disrespect of the parents finds voice through the children. Their conduct toward the grandmother emphasizes the disrespect which is characteristic of the entire family.

When the family leaves for Florida the next morning, the grandmother, against Bailey's express order forbidding it, smuggles the family cat, Pitty Sing, into the car with her because she fears it would miss her too much, or that it would accidentally asphyxiate itself if left behind. The cat does survive; ironically, however, it is responsible for the auto accident which leads to the family's death and, contrary to the grandmother's view of her importance to the cat, it befriends the man who murders the entire family. The cat alone survives.

The events leading up to the death scene itself are designed by O'Connor to display the foibles of the family and to create a sense of foreboding. Shortly after leaving Atlanta, the family passes Stone Mountain, a gigantic outcropping upon which are carved, in bas-relief, images of the long-dead heroes of an equally dead Confederacy. The grandmother, dressed so that "in case of an accident, anyone seeing her dead on the highway would know at once that she was a lady," carefully writes down the mileage of the car in anticipation of her return home. She indulges in back-seat driving, acts as a tour guide, and attempts—by citing the conduct of children in *her* time—to chastise John Wesley and June Star for their rude remarks concerning "their native states and their parents and everything else." Her fraudulent propriety is immediately undercut, however, when she calls the children's attention to a "cute little pickaninny" (a black child) standing in the door of a shack they are passing. When June Star observes the child's lack of britches, the grandmother explains that "little niggers in the country don't have the things we do."

As the children return to their comic books, we are given a number of life vs. death images which prepare us for the coming catastrophe. The grandmother takes the baby from its mother, and we see the contrast between the thin, leathery face of old age and the smooth, bland face of the baby. Immediately thereafter, the car passes "an old family burying ground," and the grandmother points out the five or six graves in it – a number equal to the occupants of the car – and mentions that it belonged to a plantation which, in response to John Wesley's question concerning its present location, has "Gone With the Wind," an answer that is doubly ironic insofar as it recalls the death of the Old South.

The children, after they finish eating the food which they brought along with them, begin to bicker, so the grandmother quiets them by telling them a story of her early courtship days. The story, which emphasizes the grandmother's failure to marry a man named Teagarden, who each Saturday afternoon brought her a watermelon, reveals both her and June Star's concern for material well-being. When June Star suggests that she would not marry a man who brought her only watermelons, the grandmother responds by replying that Mr. Teagarden purchased Coca-Cola stock and died a rich man. (For O'Connor, Coca-Cola, which was patented by a Georgia druggist, represented the height of crass commercialism.)

In addition to June Star and the grandmother, we learn that Red Sammy Butts and his wife are also concerned with the pursuit of material gain. Red Sammy regrets having allowed "two fellers" to charge gas; his wife is certain that the Misfit will "attact" the restaurant if he hears there is any money in the cash register.

The scene at The Tower cafe appears to have been designed to illustrate the depths of self-interest into which the characters have fallen. There seems to be reason, however, to suspect that the scene was created with more than surface details in mind. In an address to a group of writing students, O'Connor commented, "The kind of vision the fiction writer needs to have, or to develop, in order to increase the meaning of his story is called anagogical vision, and that is the kind of vision that is able to see different levels of reality in one image or situation."

On one level, then, The Tower may be seen as the biblical Tower where the sons of Adam had their tongues confused, "that they may not understand one another's speech." On another level, The Tower functions as a low-class greasy spoon, where the characters attempt to display their "good manners" in order to conceal their lack of concern for their fellow man. There does seem to be an inability on the part of the characters to enter into any meaningful conversation; the grandmother irritates her son by asking if he wants to dance when his wife plays "Tennessee Waltz" on the nickelodeon – which costs a dime; June Star, who has just performed a tap routine, displays her lack of manners by insulting Red Sammy's wife with the comment, "I wouldn't live in a broken-down place like this for a million bucks." The grandmother, Red Sammy, and his wife discuss the evil nature of the times and decide that, although they themselves may be good people, "a good man is hard to find." By concluding that Europe is entirely to blame for the way things are now, they successfully avoid any responsibility for the human condition.

As the family leaves The Tower, the children are again attracted to the gray monkey which attracted their attention when they first arrived. Members of the ape family have long been used in Christian art to symbolize sin, malice, cunning, and lust, and have also been used to symbolize the slothful soul of man in its blindness, greed, and sinfulness. O'Connor could hardly have selected a better symbol to epitomize the group of people gathered at The Tower than this monkey, sitting in a Chinaberry tree biting fleas between its teeth, a totally self-centered animal.

The grandmother, having fallen asleep shortly after leaving the restaurant, awakens just outside "Toomsboro" (in reality, an actual small town near Milledgeville; for purposes of the story, it functions effectively as a foreshadowing of the family's fate), where she initiates the events that will lead to the death of the family. Recalling a plantation which she visited as a young girl and which she wishes to visit again, the grandmother succeeds in getting her way by "craftily, not telling the truth but wishing she were," informing the children of a secret panel located in the house. They pester Bailey into visiting the place by kicking, screaming, and making general nuisances of themselves. It is only after they have turned down a dirt road that "looked as if no one had traveled on it in months" that the grandmother remembers that the house was *not* in Georgia but in Tennessee.

Agitated by her recollection, and fearful of Bailey's anger when he discovers her error, the grandmother jumps up and knocks over the valise which has been covering the box in which she has been secreting the forbidden cat. The cat, freed from confinement, springs onto Bailey's shoulder and remains clinging there as the car goes off the road and overturns. The children appear overjoyed at the accident, and June Star shows a complete lack of compassion for her injured mother and the shocked state of the other members of the family by announcing with disappointment, "But nobody's killed."

As if in answer to the mother's hope for a passing car, "a big black battered hearse-like automobile" appears on the top of a hill some distance away. The grandmother, by standing and waving to attract the attention of the people in the approaching car, brings down upon the family the Misfit and his two companions. It is also her identification of the Misfit which apparently causes him to decide that the family should be killed.

From this point onward, the story concerns itself with both the methodical murder of the family, and more importantly, insofar as an encounter is characteristic of much of O'Connor's fiction, with the exchange between the Misfit and the grandmother. This is an exchange which leads to her moment of epiphany.

In an address to a group of students, O'Connor noted that the grandmother "is in the most significant position life offers the Christian. She is facing death." She also noted that "the old lady is a hypocritical old soul; her wits are no match for the Misfit's nor is her capacity for grace equal to his"; and finally the grandmother realizes even in her limited way that she "is responsible for the man before her and joined to him by ties of mystery which have their roots deep in the mystery she has been prattling about so far."

It is during this confrontation that the grandmother, like the Apostle Peter, denies three times what she knows to be true when she insists that the Misfit is "a good man." The Misfit himself squelches her attempts to gain his favor by commenting, "Nome. I ain't a good man." While displaying a degree of good manners, fully the equal of those shown by the other characters in the story, the Misfit carries on a dialogue with the grandmother while his two companions, at his command, take the remainder of the family off into the woods and shoot them.

During this dialogue with the grandmother, we learn that the Misfit's father had early recognized in him an individual who would have to know "why it [life] is," and we learn that the Misfit has pondered the human condition and has reached certain conclusions concerning his experience with life. (Because of this introspection and philosophical struggling, his capacity for grace is greater than that of the hypocritical, shallow grandmother.) We learn that the Misfit has been unable to reconcile himself to the punishment he has undergone and that he has found incomprehensible the explanations of a psychiatrist (modern man's priestly substitute and a frequent target for O'Connor's satire), who has suggested that his actions are an attempt to kill his father. For him, the crime committed is of no matter "because sooner or later you're going to forget what it was you done and just be punished for it."

The grandmother's attempt to use religion as a means of escaping the death which has come to other members of her family proves to be completely unsuccessful because the Misfit, having weighed the evidence available to him, has arrived at a very definite conclusion about Jesus. " 'Jesus was the only One that ever raised the dead . . . and He shouldn't have done it. He thrown everything off balance. If He did what He said, then it's nothing for you to do but throw away everything and follow Him, and if He didn't, then it's nothing for you to do but enjoy the few minutes you got left the best way you can — by killing somebody or burning down his house or doing some other meanness to him. No pleasure but meanness,' he said and his voice had become almost a snarl."

In a final attempt to save herself, the grandmother is even willing to concede that "Maybe He didn't raise the dead," but the Misfit has already reached his conclusion. "I wasn't there so I can't say He didn't . . . if I had of been there I would of known and I wouldn't be like I am now." The Misfit, lacking the side into which he might have thrust his hand (the "proof" offered to the biblical Doubting Thomas), has clearly decided against the Christian ethic.

Finally,the grandmother's head clears for an instant, and she makes what O'Connor has called *the right gesture* and reaches out for the Misfit while commenting, "You're one of my babies. You're one of my own children." The grandmother's epiphany involves her recognition that the Misfit is, in some way, a product of the hypocritical attitudes and hollow actions which she and others like her have held and taken. They have given only lip service to spiritual concepts and have concerned themselves with the gratification of their physical and material desires in this life. The Misfit, then, represents this attitude carried to the extreme. He rejects their hypocrisy by dismissing that which they hold to be of little worth (a spiritual view of life) and concentrates on the gratification of the passions. For him, "It's nothing for you to do but enjoy the few minutes you got left."

Having been touched by grace and having recognized that she is in some way responsible for the Misfit's present condition, the grandmother, now capable of something other than concern for herself, reaches out to him in a gesture of sympathy and love. As she touches the Misfit's shoulder, he shoots her three times through the chest. As though to emphasize the changed condition of the grandmother, O'Connor provides a description of the dead body which seems to have been designed to convey the impression that the grandmother has indeed "become as a little child," a biblical admonition given to those who would obtain salvation. She "half sat and half lay in a puddle of blood with her legs crossed under her like a child's and her face smiling up at the cloudless sky."

Interestingly, the Misfit himself also appears to have experienced an epiphany as a result of these events. He—who has declared that there is "no pleasure but meanness"—decides, after having committed the ultimate meanness, "It's no real pleasure in life." This final apparent rejection of his previous view makes little sense unless one accepts O'Connor's comment on his possible future: "I don't want to equate the Misfit with the devil. I prefer to think that, however unlikely this may seem, the old lady's gesture, like the mustard seed, will grow into a great crow-filled tree in the Misfit's heart, and will be enough of a pain to him there to turn him into the prophet he was meant to become." Thus, it appears that the Misfit may have been conceived as another one of the O'Connor characters (for example, Hazel Motes and Francis Marion Tarwater—both of whom commit murders in an attempt to reject an involvement with Christ) whose "integrity lies in [their] not being . . . able to get rid of the ragged figure [Christ] who moves from tree to tree in the back of his mind" (O'Connor's Preface to the second edition of *Wise Blood*).

It is interesting to note that O'Connor includes information in the story that makes possible an alternative explanation for the grandmother's final actions in much the manner of Hawthorne, one of her favorite authors. It is not until after the accident that any part of Bailey's costume is described. At that point, we learn that "he had on a yellow sport shirt with bright blue parrots designed in it." Following Bailey's murder by Hiram and Bobby Lee, the Misfit's companions, the shirt is given to the Misfit, who dons it. Significantly, the grand-mother "couldn't name what the shirt reminded her of"; obviously, it reminded her of her son—thus, her rationale for saying, "Why, you're one of my babies." Thus, for the individual who finds "the action of grace" to be an inappropriate foundation upon which to base an ex-planation of the grandmother's conduct, it is indeed possible to argue that the grandmother, in her dizzy and panic-stricken state, literally mistakes the Misfit for one of her own children.

Although "A Good Man Is Hard to Find" is an early work in the O'Connor canon, it contains many of the elements which come to characterize the majority of her short works of fiction. Most of her stories contain an individual who has a strong feeling of self-confidence or feels that he has lived in such a way that his conduct cannot be questioned. As did the Greek tragedians, O'Connor appears to look upon these characters as being in a state of hubris (a condition characterized by overbearing pride and a sense of being beyond the rule of fate) and sees them as being ripe for catastrophe. Thus, in story after story, these individuals are brought to a crisis point in their lives, and they see their self-confidence destroyed by events, or else they experience a moment of grace which causes them to reevaluate their past lives and to see the world in a new and spiritual light. In like manner, many of the stories end in violence because O'Connor felt that it frequently took violence to awaken the self-satisfied individual to the shortcomings of his life.

THE LIFE YOU SAVE MAY BE YOUR OWN

This story may well be one of O'Connor's most humorous stories. Even though the story as it now stands appears to focus on the attempts of two equally unscrupulous characters to gain an advantage over the other, O'Connor, through the use of color imagery and somewhat obvious symbolism, manages to make the story more than merely a humorous tale. Yet it is the humor, ultimately, which first catches the attention of most readers.

Some of O'Connor's humor is similar, at least in part, to the tradition of such Old Southwest humorists (1835–1860) as Johnson J. Hooper and George W. Harris. Hooper's Simon Suggs and Harris' Sut Lovingood are both similar to O'Connor's Shiftlet. This is especially true in Shiftlet's "swapping session" scenes with Mrs. Crater. These swapping session scenes are also reminiscent of the Armsted-Snopes exchanges in the fiction of William Faulkner. Each of the major characters in O'Connor's story is aware that he, or she, has something that someone else craves, which slowly increases the apparent value of the offer until the final bargain is struck. Thus, Mrs. Crater gains, so she thinks, something to fill the void which exists on her farm (a son-in-law), while Shiftlet gains, so he thinks, his heart's desire (an automobile).

The basic plot of the story is very simple. One evening, near sunset, Tom T. Shiftlet (shiftless or shifty) arrives at the desolate and bedraggled farmhouse of Mrs. Lucynell Crater (emptiness or void) and her nearly thirty-two-year-old, deaf-mute daughter, also named Lucynell. During a conversation which allows each of the major characters to size one another up, Shiftlet, who spies an old automobile which he desires, agrees to stay on the farm in exchange for food and a place to sleep. Shiftlet is delighted to be able to sleep in the car, commenting to Mrs. Crater, "the monks of old slept in their coffins," to which she responds, "They wasn't as advanced as we are." Mrs. Crater, in making her offer, sees Shiftlet as someone who, at the least, will make repairs around the place and who, at best, is a potential husband for her daughter. Within a week, Shiftlet has made numerous repairs around the place, has taught the deaf-mute daughter to speak a single word – bird – and, to a certain extent, he has gained the trust of Mrs. Crater. He then turns his attention to the real object of his affection, the car.

Mrs. Crater, sensing an opportunity to obtain a husband for her daughter and a handyman for her farm, doles out money for a fan belt while extolling the virtues of a wife "that can't talk . . . can't sass you back or use foul language." To make her daughter appear even more attractive, Mrs. Crater even tells Shiftlet that the girl is only sixteen or seventeen. When Shiftlet succeeds in resurrecting the car, much to the delight of Lucynell who, sitting on a crate, stamps her feet and screams, "Burrdttt! bddurrddtttt!" only to be drowned out by the sound of the car, he begins to sense victory and he begins to play Mrs. Crater for all he can get. Mrs. Crater, "ravenous for a son-in-law," offers a mortgage-free farm with "a well that never runs dry" and a warm house in winter; in addition, she will even pay for paint for the auto. Shiftlet, now triumphant, extracts honeymoon money from her – first, fifteen dollars; then, seventeen-fifty – and the bargain is struck.

On the following Saturday, Shiftlet and the daughter are married while Mrs. Crater acts as witness. Leaving a somewhat distressed Mrs. Crater at the farm, the couple begin their honeymoon. Reveling in the joy of his new possession, Shiftlet drives the auto*mobile* toward Mobile (surely, an intentional pun on Shiftlet's goal), with his sense of contentment marred only when he thinks of Lucynell, the deaf-mute wife sitting next to him. About a hundred miles from the farm, he stops and abandons the sleeping Lucynell at a diner called The Hot Spot, telling the counter attendant that she is only a hitchhiker and that he needs to "make Tuscaloosa," a destination in the center of the state while Mobile is on the coast, at the extreme south edge of the state.

Perhaps somewhat depressed by his actions, and somehow influenced by the road signs which announce, "Drive carefully. The life you save may be your own," Shiftlet, feeling that ". . . a man with a car had a responsibility to others," stops and picks up a young boy who is hitchhiking. Evidently convinced that the boy has run away from home, Shiftlet begins to extol the virtues of his "old mother" whom he supposedly left. As Shiftlet becomes more eloquent, warming to the new role which he has created for himself (advisor to the wayward and misdirected), the boy, in apparent disgust and perhaps sensing Shiftlet's hypocrisy, condemns all mothers in general and leaps from the slowly moving car. Briefly shocked, Shiftlet offers up a short prayer and then races an approaching shower into Mobile.

Since this is one of O'Connor's shorter stories, it provides an excellent opportunity to examine in some detail the techniques which she developed in order to provide an anagogical level of meaning to her stories. Drawing on the definitions laid down by the medieval interpreters of the scriptures, O'Connor noted, "The kind of vision the fiction writer needs to have, or develop, in order to increase the meaning of his story is called anagogical vision, and that is the kind of vision that is able to see different levels of reality in one image or situation." After continuing her discussion, in which she considers two other kinds of interpretation used by the medieval commentators – the allegorical and the tropological, she continues, ". . . one they called anagogical, which had to do with the Divine life and our participation in it . . . was also an attitude toward all creation, and a way of reading nature which included most possibilities, and I think it is this enlarged view of the human scene that the fiction writer has to cultivate if he is ever going to write stories that have any chance of becoming a permanent part of our literatures."

O'Connor regularly uses color imagery, analogies, and traditional symbolic techniques to create the double vision which she considered so important to her fiction. If one examines those elements as they are used in this story, it becomes, as we have said, more than a humorous tale; it becomes a comment on at least one of the ways by which man may separate himself from the Divine order of things.

The color imagery used in the story provides considerable insight into O'Connor's intentions. We note that Shiftlet arrives at the farm wearing a black suit and a brown hat. Black has traditionally been viewed as a symbol of physical death and of the underworld, while brown is associated with spiritual death and degradation. Gray, the color of the hats of Mrs. Crater and the young hitchhiker, as well as of the turnip-shaped cloud which descends over the sun at the end of the story, has been variously associated with neutralization, egoism, depression, inertia, and indifference. While the hat is the only item of Mrs. Crater's clothing to be described, O'Connor pays particular attention to the clothing worn by the daughter. The color imagery associated with her is designed to emphasize her purity and innocence, as well as to associate her with the divine. Blue, the color of her dress when we first see her, and of her eyes, is associated with heaven and heavenly love and has become the traditional color associated with the Virgin Mary in Christian art. The white of her wedding dress is, of course, usually representative of innocence and purity while the "pink-gold hair" may be seen as emblematic of the divine (gold) residing in the flesh (pink). Green, the color which Shiftlet paints the car, while emblematic of vegetation and spring, has also been considered suggestive of charity and the regeneration of the soul through good works. Yellow, the color of the band which he paints over the green, and of the fat moon which appears in the branches of the fig tree, is frequently used to suggest infernal light, degradation, betrayal, treason, and deceit. Finally, the sun, given a color only late in the story, is described as a "reddening ball"; red, normally associated with blood, passion, creativity, has also been adopted by the Church as the color for martyred saints. A careful examination of O'Connor's use of color will generally give an indication of the direction in which she wished to point the reaction of her readers.

In addition to her use of color imagery, O'Connor also provides a number of traditional symbols which help to clarify her intent in the story. Shiftlet arrives at the Crater farm at sunset, and Mrs. Crater finds it necessary to shield her eyes from the piercing sun in order to see him. Traditional associations of the sun with the eye of God or the wordplay of sun/son help explain O'Connor's use of sun imagery at both the beginning and end of the story. Standing with his good arm and his stump outstretched against the sunset, Shiftlet's "figure formed a crooked cross," an indication that, although in the light of the sun/son he may appear as a distortion of that most basic of Christian symbols, he is still created in that image. By the end of the story, however, he and his prayer are separated from the sun by the gray, turnip-shaped cloud, an indication that as a result of his egoism and his indifference, he has rejected the grace offered him in the form of the innocent Lucynell and a farm which he could tend. Grace, as you may recall from our discussion of it in the section on O'Connor's view of her writing, is the supernatural aid given to man which allows him new insight into his relationship with the divine scheme of things. Man, having free will, may, however, choose *not* to act on this new insight.

Shiftlet's interest in the mystery of life, his occupation as a carpenter, and his claim that he has "a moral intelligence," all suggest that in the first third of the story, at least, he is in a position to either accept or reject an offer of grace. By the end of the second third of the story, he has made his choice, and we are told that his "smile stretched like a weary snake waking up by a fire." The final third of the story then is used to show the results of his choice, and we see him cut off from the sun/son, racing a shower into Mobile. The car which Shiftlet has likened to the spirit—". . . the spirit, lady, is like an automobile: always on the move, always . . ."—becomes, in a very real sense, the coffin which claims his soul. Thus, the car painted green, emblematic of the regeneration of the soul through good works, is given a yellow stripe indicating that Shiftlet has betrayed his opportunity for grace.

That Lucynell is intended to function as the instrument of Shiftlet's salvation is made obvious by both the color imagery and the symbols associated with her. As the three ride into town for the marriage ceremony, we note that every once in a while Lucynell's "placid expression was changed by a sly isolated thought like a shoot of green in the desert." Even the description of "her eyes as blue as a peacock's neck" uses the color blue, associated with heavenly love. In addition, the peacock, in Christian iconography a symbol of immortality, is used in a simile to reinforce other symbols indicating her function in the story. Mrs. Crater's comment that she wouldn't give Lucynell "for a casket of jewels" illustrates the double-edged nature of O'Connor's imagery and the precision with which she tends to write. In regard to Shiftlet, Lucynell becomes the pearl of great price which Christ likens to the kingdom of heaven in Matthew 13:45 ("a merchant . . . when he found one pearl of great price, went and sold all that he had and bought it"). In regard to Mrs. Crater, she becomes the pearl which Christ describes in the Sermon on the Mount in Matthew 7:6 ("neither cast ye your pearls before swine, lest they trample them under their feet").

You might also note that O'Connor uses the word "casket" rather than "chest" or "box" of jewels, thereby echoing the coffin imagery associated with the car. This helps link Mrs. Crater with Shiftlet, both pursuing material goals and both surrendering the spiritual goal represented by the innocent Lucynell, actions which, from O'Connor's point of view, lead man to spiritual death. As Shiftlet and Lucynell are driving toward Mobile, she is described as picking the decorative wooden cherries from the brim of her hat and throwing them, one by one, out of the window. The cherry, in Christian art, has been associated with the sweetness of character derived from good works or with the delights of the blessed. Finally, according to the young counterman in The Hot Spot, "She looks like an angel of Gawd."

This analysis of the story relies upon a general understanding of O'Connor's point of view concerning her fiction. It is not, however, the only way that the story may be read. Some critics are entranced by the humor in the story and pay little attention to the color imagery and the underlying religious meaning which the story contains. At least one critic has suggested that Mr. Shiftlet was intended to represent a Christ figure, while others have seen him as a Satanic figure. Certainly the story has, as does all good literature, a rich enough texture to support a number of ways of looking at it. More importantly, however, one should remember a piece of advice which O'Connor gave a group of would-be writers: "When anyone asks what a story is about, the only proper thing is to tell him to read the story. The meaning of fiction is not abstract meaning but experienced meaning, and the purpose of making statements about the meaning of a story is only to help you to experience that meaning more fully."

THE RIVER

In this story, which is one of O'Connor's early works, her use of color imagery and her use of symbols are already well developed. The story is told from an omniscient point-of-view and covers a two-day span in the life of the main character, Harry Ashfield. Harry is about four or five years old, and he is the only child of an urban family which has little time to spend with him. His family occupies their time by giving parties and sleeping late the following day.

As the story opens, Harry is being prepared by his father to go off with a sitter, Mrs. Connin. She is a backwoods religious fundamentalist who believes in faith healing. Harry's mother is suffering from a hangover and remains in bed. Because his father is hardly awake at six o'clock in the morning, he pushes the boy into the hall without having properly dressed him. When Mrs. Connin complains that Harry "ain't fixed right," his father replies, "Well then for Christ's sake fix him." Little does he realize that that will be just what Mrs. Connin will do—that is, she will "fix" Harry "right," for Christ's sake.

As Harry and Mrs. Connin are riding the trolley to the outskirts of town, she tells him about the faith healer they are going to see, an itinerant preacher named Bevel Summers. Harry, starved for affection, succeeds in gaining Mrs. Connin's attention by claiming that his own name is also Bevel.

When Harry arrives at the Connin farm, he discovers that the world of the farm is quite different from the world he knows at home. "You found out more when you left where you lived," he realizes. Almost immediately, the Connin boys trick him into letting a pig out of the pigpen, and it knocks Harry over. He quickly learns that real pigs are not pink with curly tails and bow-ties, but, instead, that they are gray and sour looking. He also discovers that he "had been made by a carpenter named Jesus Christ," and not by a doctor named Sladewall. Harry concludes that the Sladewall story must be a joke because his own family "joked a lot." The pictures on the wall of the Connin home are of real people—not the abstract watercolor he knows at home. He is even convinced that the pictures in a book called *The*

Life of Jesus Christ for Readers Under Twelve must be accurate because it shows pictures of real pigs—not drawings of cute, storybook pigs.

While the Connin family goes off to the river to attend the healing service, they take Harry/Bevel along with them. He is then taken from Mrs. Connin by the preacher, and Harry realizes that "this was no joke. Where he lived everything was a joke." After Harry is baptized, the preacher tells him that he now "counts."

Mrs. Connin returns Harry to the city that evening, and when they arrive, another party is in progress. This section of the story is designed to reinforce the feeling of alienation from which Harry/Bevel suffers because of his family life, and it also provides much of the humor of the story. Particularly telling is the scene in which his mother puts him to bed, and he hears her voice coming from a long way away, "as if he were under the river and she on top of it."

On Monday morning, Harry awakens, finds something to eat, and entertains himself by dumping a few ashtrays onto the floor. His parents are still asleep, and he is convinced that they will "be out cold until one o'clock." When he notices that his shoes are still damp, he begins to think about the river and suddenly "he knew what he wanted to do." He takes a trolley token from his mother's purse, leaves the apartment, and returns to the river. There, determined to baptize himself and "to keep on going . . . until he found the Kingdom of Christ in the river," he jumps into the river and drowns.

A number of critics have difficulty with this story because they feel Harry's death serves no purpose. O'Connor, however, was careful to create a character whose youth places him below the age of accountability—in the Catholic faith, that age is seven years old. Since Harry has been baptized and cannot be held accountable for his actions, he dies a good death. O'Connor, in fact, once noted that Harry "comes to a good end. He's saved from those nutty parents, a fate worse than death. He's been baptized and so he goes to his Maker; this is a good end."

A LATE ENCOUNTER WITH THE ENEMY

This story appears to have been inspired by an article and a picture which appeared in the *Milledgeville Union Recorder* in August of 1951. The story deals with the appearance of General William J. Bush at a graduation ceremony at Georgia College. At that time, he was more than one hundred years old and was quoted as saying, "I'm getting younger every day. My hair is just now fixing to turn black." The General lived to be one hundred and seven years old before he died at his home in Fitzgerald, Georgia.

O'Connor uses the first portion of her story to describe the characters and to establish the basic irony of their situations. Both old George Poker Sash (based presumably on General Bush) and his granddaughter, Sally Poker Sash, are individuals who live for the gratification of their own desires. Sally Poker Sash, who is sixty-two years old, has prayed that her grandfather, who is a hundred and four years old, will live until she is able to graduate from college with a B.S. degree in education. She has attended summer school each year for the past twenty years, and she fears that she "might be cheated out of her triumph because she so often was." Her goal is to have her grandfather on stage when she receives her degree in order to show "what all was behind her and not behind them" (a reference to "all the upstarts who had . . . unsettled the ways of decent living"). Similarly, old George Poker Sash is willing "to sit on stage in his uniform so that they could see him." At heart, however, he is bored by all processions (including graduation processions); he would much rather be the center of attention at a parade.

As you read through this story, you should pay special attention to O'Connor's repeated use of images which function to tie the elements of the story together and to foreshadow the ending. In particular, note O'Connor's reference in the first paragraph of the story to the River Styx (in Greek mythology, this is the river across which dead souls were ferried to the Underworld by the boatman Charon). O'Connor's frequent use of the phrase "black procession" in this story suggests the approach of death and all those things associated with it, and Sally Poker Sash's dream of having her grandfather silently revered and honored in the hearts of the graduation audience foreshadows a major disappointment in her life.

For both Sally Poker Sash and old George Poker Sash, the most memorable event in both their lives was a premiere which they attended twelve years earlier in Atlanta. It was then that "General Tennessee Flintrock Sash of the Confederacy" had been created by the Hollywood publicity agents. We are told that, in reality, Sally's grandfather was probably no more than a foot soldier during the Civil War, even though Sally claims that he was a Major.

The memory of this false, artificial reality has become a focal point in the lives of both old "General" George Poker Sash and Sally. For the General, it was a moment of triumph, and he constantly relives that experience – at the risk of being made aware of the real nature of his life. For Sally Poker, the moment of triumph in Atlanta turned to tragedy, however, for she went on stage without changing from her brown "Girl Scout oxfords" into the silver slippers which she had purchased to compliment her long, glamorous black crepe gown. That careless mistake, she believes, will finally be redeemed by the presence of her famous grandfather on stage for her graduation.

On the day of Sally's graduation, everything goes well – until she discovers that her nephew, John Wesley, did *not* take her grandfather onto the stage as she directed him to do. Instead, he allowed the old man to sit in the hot sun while he himself stopped to drink a Coca-Cola. At this point, the old General felt "as if there were a little hole beginning to widen in the top of his head." This "hole," of course, is a precursor of his death. Remember that earlier, we were told that he could not possibly conceive of death – "living had got to be such a habit with him."

Finally, as the old General sits on the stage, he attempts to ignore the speakers; however, he is unable to do so because of the ever-widening "hole" that he feels in his head. The comments of one of the speakers, you should note, are of importance because they echo one of O'Connor's major themes in this story: "If we forget our past . . . we won't remember our future and it will be as well for we won't have one."

From O'Connor's point of view, the events of a person's lifetime are properly understood only when one sees them against the background of the Divine scheme – a scheme which extends from the time of Creation to the Last Judgment. By remembering his Fall from Eden and God's promise of a future opportunity for redemption, man can be led to remember the promise of salvation which is made available through the sacrifice of Christ (Hebrews 1:2). The old General, having forgotten his real past, which includes his family, as well as his wartime experiences, attempts to recall his finest moment of glory: "He tried to see himself and the horse mounted in the middle of a float full of beautiful girls, being driven slowly through downtown Atlanta." He is unable to conjure up this "vision," however, because he is too distracted by the speaker's words.

The General's moment of epiphany and his death occur as the graduates move forward to receive their diplomas. In his final moments, during his moment of epiphany, his recognition of his true past comes flooding in on him, "as if the past were the only future now and he had to endure it." The "black procession," now an image of his impending death, appears to be almost upon him, and he recognizes it because "it had been dogging all his days." He dies while trying desperately to "see over" the black procession in order to "find out what comes after the past."

The General's epiphany appears to serve two purposes in the story. First, it reinforces the commencement speaker's view that the ability to "remember the future" is conditioned by one's ability to remember the past. The General has chosen to remember a false, culturally created past, and he dies before the memory of his true past can lead him to a knowledge of the future. From O'Connor's point of view, those who accept a false past as true and then attempt to make its preservation the focus of their lives, have little chance of finding a spiritually satisfying afterlife.

The second purpose of the General's epiphanal moment stresses the mortality of all things. As it must come to all men, death comes to the General, who has forgotten its inevitability. In the orthodox religious view, life must be a preparation for death; to live while attempting only to preserve the great moments of the past is to abandon all hope for the future. Thus, one ends one's life by trying vainly, as did the General, "to find out what comes after the past."

Although Sally Poker Sash does not experience an epiphany in the story, O'Connor arranges the details in such a way that it appears impossible for her to avoid one. When she realizes that her moment of triumph (receiving her scroll at graduation) occurs after her grandfather dies (symbolically, a dead past which she refuses to relinquish), her nightmare comes true. The consequent destruction of her pride may, then, be viewed as a necessary step which will turn her attention from her old concerns; indeed, it may well be the beginning of a new realization of the purpose for her existence.

The story ends with a twist reminiscent of some of O. Henry's best short stories. After the graduation ceremony, the Boy Scout nephew who was in charge of General Sash "bumped him out the back way and rolled him at high speed down a flagstone path and was waiting now, with the corpse, in the long line at the Coca-Cola machine." This final tableau leaves one with an image of a dead past juxtaposed with a representative of the new generation – a generation which is caught up in the rush to satisfy its physical/material needs from one of O'Connor's archetypal, despised images of modern culture, a Coca-Cola machine. Given her tendency to deal with anagogical meanings, one might see this vision as O'Connor's way of rejecting both the old *and* the new (neither of which provides an answer to the General's final question) as bastions behind which man might hide himself.

THE DISPLACED PERSON

As we noted in discussing "A Good Man Is Hard to Find," O'Connor was able to make use of events which occurred around Milledgeville or else were reported in the newspapers and magazines which she read. The first version of "The Displaced Person" appears to have been at least partly inspired by two incidents; first, by a 1949 newspaper story about the Jeryczuks (a refugee family), who had settled on a dairy farm near Milledgeville; and second, by the arrival of a refugee family in 1951, who were hired to work at Andalusia, O'Connor's mother's dairy farm. In a letter to her friends Sally and Robert Fitzgerald, O'Connor reported that "Mrs. P.," the wife of the dairyman who worked for Mrs. O'Connor, asked, "Do you think they'll [the refugees] know what colors even is?"

This sentence and the incident which provoked it (the making of curtains from different colored feed sacks for the tenant house) were moved almost verbatim into the story. Even Mr. Shortley's comment, "I ain't going to have the Pope of Rome tell me how to run no dairy," appears to have its origins in events which occurred in September of 1951. In another letter to the Fitzgeralds, O'Connor writes, "They are having conventions all over the place and making resolutions and having the time of their lives. You'd think the Pope was about to annex the Sovereign State of Georgia."

The first version of "The Displaced Person," published in 1954, concentrates on Mrs. Shortley's growing fear of and hatred for the Guizacs and the unknown culture and religion which they represent. Mrs. Shortley associates the Guizacs with the victims of the World War II death camps, pictures of which she saw in local newsreels; she fears that the Guizacs might be capable of committing the same acts of violence against others. She even imagines that the priest who arranges for the Guizacs to come to the farm is an evil force who came "to plant the Whore of Babylon in the midst of the righteous." (Some fundamentalist religious groups commonly refer to the Roman Catholic Church as the Whore of Babylon.)

Because Mr. Guizac proves to be a much better worker than Mr.

Shortley, Mrs. McIntyre tells the priest that she has decided to give the Shortleys a month's notice. Mrs. Shortley overhears this conversation and orders her family to pack. As they are leaving the following dawn, Mrs. Shortley dies of a heart attack in the car.

O'Connor describes Mrs. Shortley's death by suggesting that Mrs. Shortley's vision of her "true country" (the afterlife) might be coming from "inside her"; then, O'Connor further depicts Mrs. Shortley's death by using the same imagery which Mrs. Shortley associated with the death camps in Europe – a confused intermingling of body parts and piles of corpses. There is a certain irony in O'Connor's noting that the Shortley girls do not realize that their mother has undergone a "great experience" or has been "displaced in the world from all that belonged to her." It is also ironic that it is Mr. Guizac, the frail, foreign, displaced person, who displaces the mountainous Mrs. Shortley and who serves as the catalyst which forces her to "contemplate for the first time the tremendous frontiers of her true country."

By describing Mrs. Shortley in the first paragraph of the 1954 version of the story as having a stomach upon which the sign "DAMNATION TO THE EVIL-DOER. YOU WILL BE UNCOVERED" might have been painted, O'Connor leads the reader to recall the words of Christ in the seventh chapter of Matthew: "God will judge you in the same way you judge others, and he will apply to you the same rules you apply to others."

The conclusion of the story, then, suggests that Mrs. Shortley has received her just reward and has been uncovered as the evil-doer standing in danger of damnation. O'Connor, however, was obviously not satisfied to let the story end here because she expanded and changed the focus of the story before it was published as the final selection in her first volume of short stories.

The addition of all the references to the peacock, the few lines needed to prepare the reader for the displaced person's attempt to marry his cousin to the Negro Sulk, and the few minor stylistic modifications which O'Connor made are the only changes which she made in the original story in order to integrate it into the longer version. Although the changes may appear minor, the manner in which they are handled produces a profound change in the tone of the story.

The 1954 version of the story begins, "Mrs. Shortley . . ."; the final version begins, "The peacock . . ." O'Connor once noted that the peacock represents the eyes of the Church, but one does not need to be familiar with O'Connor's particular point of view in order to appreciate the image of the peacock in the story.

For centuries, the peacock has been associated with immortality and has been employed as one of the standard symbols within the Christian tradition. In the second paragraph of the story, we see the peacock's attention "fixed in the distance on something no one else could see." Any reader who realizes that this image is associated with that of the sun/son "which was creeping behind a ragged wall of cloud as if it pretended to be an intruder," and realizes that it is ignored by Mrs. Shortley, "the giant wife of the countryside, come out at some sign of danger to see what the trouble was," will, if he is familiar with O'Connor's fiction, know that he is about to be treated to another story in which the profane world is to be penetrated by the sacred.

In the final version of the story, Mrs. Shortley is the first human character introduced, and it is through her eyes that we perceive the initial sequence of events. Consequently, we come to know her as O'Connor uses her character to establish the setting of the story and to outline the social order which Mr. Guizac will disrupt.

The dairy farm is owned by Mrs. McIntyre, thus putting her at the top of the miniature society. Mrs. Shortley sees herself as next in line because she knows that Mrs. McIntyre would not talk to her about "poor white trash" if she considered Mrs. Shortley to be trashy. Mr. Shortley, who had "never in his life doubted her omniscience," stands next in the hierarchy, followed by the Shortley children, and then by the two black workers, Astor and Sulk.

It is a society which has learned to function smoothly because all of its members have tacitly agreed to overlook the corruption of the other members in exchange for their overlooking others' corruption. Both Mr. Shortley and the Negroes operate illegal stills but "there had never been any disagreeableness between them" because they all know and abide by their tacit agreement. When Mr. Guizac, not a member of this society, catches the young Negro, Sulk, stealing a turkey, Mrs. McIntyre has to go to great lengths to explain to him that "all Negroes would steal," and the incident is dropped.

Mrs. Shortley, "the giant wife of the countryside," is primarily concerned with preserving the sanctity of her position and with maintaining the stability of her small domain. Her mental limitations are such that she cannot understand the special circumstances of the poor refugees from Europe, and she considers them to be "only hired help," like her family and the Negroes. Because she is a woman of determination, self-confidence, and limited perception, she cannot imagine that she and her family will be the ones displaced by the Guizacs.

Consequently, when Mr. Guizac proves to be an admirable worker and impresses Mrs. McIntyre with his ability, Mrs. Shortley, feeling her society threatened, tells her husband, "I aim to take up for the niggers when the time comes." She even holds back a secret which she feels "would floor Mrs. McIntyre" and restore everything to normalcy. However, when she overhears Mrs. McIntyre tell the priest that the Shortleys will be given a month's notice, her world crumbles and she dies shortly thereafter.

With the introduction of the peacock in the final version of the story, O'Connor is able to provide a way of ranking the spiritual level of her major characters. She does this by noting their reaction to the peacock who "stood still as if he had just come down from some sun-drenched height to be a vision for them all." For the priest, who functions as the touchstone against which Mrs. McIntyre and Mrs. Shortley are measured, the peacock is a "beauti-ful birdrrrd," with "a tail full of suns." Later, the priest is "transfixed" when the peacock suddenly spreads its tail; he comments, "Christ will come like that," and later, he observes the peacock and murmurs, "The Transfiguration."

To Mrs. Shortley, "religion was essentially for those who didn't have the brains to avoid evil without it," and thus the bird was "nothing but a peachicken." Even when the tail of the bird with its all-seeing eyes is placed directly before her and the reader is informed that Mrs. Shortley "might have been looking at a map of the universe," she stands with unseeing eyes because "she was having an inner vision instead." It is only after Mrs. McIntyre has announced, concerning Mr. Guizac, "That man is my salvation," that Mrs. Shortley turns to religion and allows her inner vision to lead her to prophesy: "The children of wicked nations will be butchered." Her prophecy continues with a description of the dislocation of body parts, a reference to a newsreel footage she has seen. Ironically, it is Mrs. Shortley's death – not the death of Mr. Guizac – which closely resembles the "inner vision" which she has been given.

For Mrs. McIntyre, who tells the priest, "I'm not theological, I'm practical," the peacock serves to remind her of her marriage to the Judge, her first husband. Although when he died, he left only a bankrupt estate, O'Connor tells us that the three years that he lived after

he and Mrs. McIntyre were married were "the happiest and most pros-
perous of Mrs. McIntyre's life." The gradual decline of the flock marks
the decline of Mrs. McIntyre's ability to love anyone or anything for
itself; but the very fact that she has kept the peafowl around, if for
no more than "a superstitious fear of annoying the Judge in his grave,"
aligns her more closely with the priest rather than with the Shortleys.
In addition, even though her motive for accepting Mr. Guizac may
be primarily economic, and even though she may not understand him,
she does *not* have the irrational hatred of the Guizacs which marks
the attitude of the Shortleys.

If Part I of the story belongs to Mrs. Shortley, the second half
belongs to Mrs. McIntyre, and O'Connor then further subdivides
Part II of the story into two halves. The first half of Part II is used
to develop Mrs. McIntyre's character; the second half of Part II is
used to reveal the secret which Mrs. Shortley felt "would floor Mrs.
McIntyre."

To develop Mrs. McIntyre's character, O'Connor uses an extended
conversation between her and the old Negro, Astor. The character
of Astor was based, as she wrote to a friend, on an old Negro employee
of her mother. "The old man is 84 but vertical or more or less so. He
doesn't see too good and the other day he fertilized some of my
mother's bulbs with worm medicine for the calves." Her personal affection for this old man may be one factor which helps to account for
the fact that his character is not present at the moment of Guizac's
accident. In terms of the story, he is the only other person on the
farm who remembers the Judge, and he has seen the change in Mrs.
McIntyre, a change marked by the steadily declining number of peafowl on the farm and by a steadily increasing materialism on the part
of Mrs. McIntyre.

In the second half of Part II, Mrs. McIntyre learns that Mr. Guizac
has been receiving money from Sulk, the younger Negro worker on
the farm. The money is to be used to pay half of the fare needed to
bring Mr. Guizac's female cousin to America. In exchange for that
financial help, the cousin is to become Sulk's wife.

The secret which Mrs. Shortley had been keeping to herself does
indeed "floor" Mrs. McIntyre. She goes into the house, takes to her
bed, and presses her "hand over her heart as if she were trying to
keep it in place." Mrs. McIntyre is made of sterner stuff than Mrs.
Shortley, though, and in a few moments, she decides that "They're

all the same," a reference to all the irresponsible hired help she has had in the past.

Following a brief cry, she retires to the back hall, the place where the Judge's old desk is located. "It was a kind of memorial to him, sacred because he had conducted his business there." As if to emphasize Mrs. McIntyre's worship of material things, O'Connor describes the room as being "dark and quiet as a chapel." The desk has a "small safe, empty but locked, set like a tabernacle in the center of it." (In Roman Catholic churches and in a number of Eastern churches, the tabernacle is the focal point of the altar because it is the receptacle which houses the Host, the communion bread, used during the Mass.) By using this scene, O'Connor manages to describe both the physical poverty and the spiritual poverty of Mrs. McIntyre. A few minutes later, moving "as if she had gained some strength," she drives to the cornfield to confront Mr. Guizac.

Mrs. McIntyre's confrontation with Mr. Guizac is prefaced and concluded by O'Connor's use of graveyard imagery. We see Mr. Guizac cutting silage "from the outside of the field in a circular path to the center where the graveyard was," and at the end of section two of Part II, we are told that by nightfall, Mr. Guizac will have worked his way to the center of the field "where the Judge lay grinning under his desecrated monument." Mrs. McIntyre, her arms folded (an image which connects her with Mrs. Shortley), waits until Mr. Guizac comes over to her and then she produces the picture which she took from Sulk. She informs Mr. Guizac that he cannot bring the girl to America and marry her to a Negro. "Maybe it can be done in Poland but it can't be done here and you'll have to stop." You should note at this point that her first appeal is based on the assumption that a person cannot overturn the rules governing traditions and the organization of the small society of which she is the head. Mr. Guizac, thinking that the problem may be the young age of the girl in the picture, tells Mrs. McIntyre that the picture is an old one and that the girl is now sixteen. She then threatens to dismiss him if he mentions the girl again to Sulk.

As Mr. Guizac struggles to understand Mrs. McIntyre's objections, she recalls one of the poisonous comments made by Mrs. Shortley, who had insisted that Guizac understood everything and only pretended not to "so as to do exactly as he pleases." Mr. Guizac's suggestion that "She no care black. . . . She in camp three year" causes Mrs.

McIntyre to shift her argument. By claiming that the place is *hers* and by stating firmly that she is *not responsible* for the world's misery, Mrs. McIntyre moves away from what O'Connor would have considered a proper response. Man, according to Christian tradition, is placed as a caretaker of this world only, not as an owner of it; just as we bring nothing into this world, it is equally certain that we take nothing from it. More importantly, however, Mrs. McIntyre has failed to extend proper charity to Mr. Guizac, ignoring the admonition of Christ, "Whatsoever ye do unto the least of these my brethren, ye do unto me."

Part II of the story closes on an ambivalent note, with Mrs. McIntyre described as standing and looking out at Mr. Guizac "as if she were watching him through a gunsight," and, later, she stands with her arms folded "as if she were equal to anything." Mrs. McIntyre is, however, also described as having "an aging cherubic face" and a heart "beating as if some interior violence had already been done to her." The cherubic face image appears to be used to tie her to the "naked granite cherub" which the Judge brought home "partly because its face had reminded him of his wife," a woman whom the Judge realized at once "admired him for himself." The cherub had been placed on the Judge's grave and, later, it was stolen by one of the tenant families Mrs. McIntyre had hired. "Mrs. McIntyre had never been able to afford to have it replaced," a possible indication that her concern for others has been replaced by materialistic considerations. The folded-arm image, which we earlier associated with Mrs. Shortley, and the gunsight image appear to be used as foreshadowing images.

The final section of the story, until the death of Mr. Guizac, continues to focus on Mrs. McIntyre's inner conflict with Mr. Guizac. Although she marshals many arguments to demonstrate that Mr. Guizac "doesn't fit in" and that she herself is under "no legal obligation" to keep him, she is unable to bring herself to dismiss Mr. Guizac because he is an extremely capable worker and because the priest has suggested that she has a moral obligation to keep him. "She felt she must have this out with the priest before she fired the Displaced Person."

Although Mrs. McIntyre's confrontations with the priest and Mr. Shortley's conversations with Sulk add a note of humor to Mrs. McIntyre's conflict, you should not overlook the serious undercurrent which is at play throughout this final section of the story. Clearly, the priest points the way toward salvation, and just as clearly, Mr. Shortley points the way toward the road to damnation.

Although Mrs. McIntyre finally tells the priest, "as far as I'm concerned . . . Christ was just another D.P.," she still cannot bring herself to fire Guizac, and the outer manifestation of her inner struggle is perfectly clear to Mr. Shortley, who notices that "she looked as if something were wearing her down from the inside." At least part of Mrs. McIntyre's difficulty comes because "she had never discharged anyone before; they had all left her."

Finally, driven by a dream in which she sees herself overcoming the priest's objections and insisting that Mr. Guizac is just "one too many," Mrs. McIntyre decides to give Guizac his month's notice. The following morning, however, she goes to the barn, but she is still unable to fire the Pole and so she settles for the assertion, "This is my place. . . . All of you are extra."

Mr. Shortley's role in the story is made unmistakably clear at this point. While Mrs. McIntyre is talking to Mr. Guizac, "she saw a long beak-nosed shadow slide like a snake halfway up the sunlit open door and stop." Because Mrs. McIntyre failed to fire the Pole, Mr. Shortley takes his case to the people of the town. "Since he didn't have Mrs. Shortley to do the talking any more, he had started doing it himself and had found that he had a gift for it. He had the power of making other people see his logic" (like the serpent in Eden, perhaps). When Mrs. McIntyre discovers that everyone in town knows Mr. Shortley's version of her business and that everyone is "critical of her conduct," she convinces herself that she has "a moral obligation" to fire Mr. Guizac.

The following morning, she goes out to fire Guizac, and O'Connor tells us that "the countryside seemed to be receding from the little circle of noise around the shed." This description appears designed to cause the reader to recall "the sky full of white fish [frequently used as a symbol of Christ] carried lazily on their sides" (therefore, dead or belly up), and pieces of the sun "washed in the opposite direction," which appear on the Sunday afternoon that Mrs. Shortley has her inner vision of butchery. In both instances, nature is seen to draw back from the evil which is about to occur.

As she stands waiting for Sulk and Mr. Shortley to get "out of the way" before she begins "her unpleasant duty," Mrs. McIntyre becomes a witness to—and an accomplice in—the death of Mr. Guizac: he is killed in a tractor accident which she witnesses. Later, she remembers that "she had started to shout to the Displaced Person but that she had not. She had felt her eyes and Mr. Shortley's eyes and the Negro's eyes come together in one look that froze them in collusion forever," and then she fainted.

After she comes to, Mrs. McIntyre sees the priest give Mr. Guizac final communion, but "her mind was not taking hold of all that was happening. She felt she was in some foreign country where the people bent over the body were natives, and she watched like a stranger while the dead man was carried away in the ambulance."

Mr. Guizac's death destroys both Mrs. McIntyre's farm and her health. All of her help leaves, and she is hospitalized with "a nervous affliction." Upon her return home, she is forced to sell all her cattle at a loss and retire to live on "what she had, while she tried to save her declining health." Paradoxically, it is the loss of the material things which she valued too highly that appears to open the door to her spiritual well-being. Although the story does not end with her conversion, the circumstances which surround her suggest that in her chastened condition, it cannot be long in coming. Left in the care of an old black woman, she is rarely visited by anyone but the old priest who comes once a week to feed bread crumbs to the peacock and then comes into the house to "sit by the side of her bed and explain the doctrines of the Church."

Some critics have found "The Displaced Person" to be less effective than many of O'Connor's other stories because they feel that it contains a structural weakness caused by her addition of the last two sections of the story. Although we may readily admit that this story is, like any other story of merit, open to any number of different interpretations, an examination of what O'Connor called "the added dimension" (the anagogical intent) of the story shows it to be much more unified than some critics have chosen to admit. Therefore, let us look briefly at what appears to be the added dimension of this story.

As the final story in her first collection, *A Good Man Is Hard to Find and Other Stories,* one might reasonably expect to find an example of a truly "good man" in it. That good man is, of course, Mr. Guizac, the Displaced Person. He, however, is not the only person displaced in this story. At the end of Part I, Mrs. Shortley is "displaced in the world from all that belonged to her." At the end of the story, Mrs. McIntyre feels as if she is "in some foreign country" where she is a stranger. By his death, Mr. Guizac is displaced from his new home, and by the end of the story, all those attached to the McIntyre farm have been dispersed. Assuming, then, that the story deals with the human person displaced, one can observe a unity within the story which explains it within the framework of O'Connor's world view.

Mrs. Shortley, the ignorant and self-centered enemy of Mr. Guizac, distorts both the countryside and religion to serve her purposes. She is hardly "the faithful servant" for she takes advantage of her employer, and she shows no compassion for those less fortunate than herself. By extension, of course, Mr. Shortley is a part of his wife's world. That her ultimate destination appears to be damnation should come as no surprise to the reader.

Mr. Guizac, on the other hand, is the model of "the faithful servant"; he toils diligently for his employer, and he shows compassion for his fellow beings, as illustrated by his attempt to bring his cousin to America. At his death, he receives communion, and the assumption is that his end is a good one.

The case of Mrs. McIntyre is much more ambiguous. During the course of the story, we see her being driven by materialistic greed; but during the Judge's lifetime, she was happy, and he associated her with the granite cherub. But Mrs. McIntyre partakes of many of the negative aspects of Mrs. Shortley. She is self-centered and vain, although she is not as ignorant and as suspicious of the Guizacs as Mrs. Shortley is. Mrs. McIntyre cannot bring herself to fire Mr. Guizac; instead, she becomes a quiet conspirator in his death.

When one concentrates on the anagogical level of the story, it would appear that O'Connor has presented the consequences of human conduct in a world where all men are displaced from the home which was originally intended for them. Mrs. Shortley is condemned, Mrs. McIntyre is shown undergoing a kind of living purgatory, and Mr. Guizac, as a good man, is presumably granted a spiritual reward for his faithful service.

THE ARTIFICIAL NIGGER

On more than one occasion, O'Connor wrote to friends that her favorite story, among those she had written, was "The Artificial Nigger" and that it was ". . . probably the best thing I'll ever write." Although she wrote to another friend, "My disposition is a combination of Nelson's and Hulga's" (the protagonist of "Good Country People"), her satisfaction with the story appears not to have stemmed from her likeness to one of the characters in the story but from her conviction that it was one story in which she had successfully and plainly shown the action of grace bringing about a definite change of attitude in one of her characters.

Since O'Connor reported that she took two or three months to write "The Artificial Nigger" (as opposed to about four days for "Good Country People"), you should expect to find it particularly rich in imagery and allusion. Although we cannot examine in detail all of those possible references in this short account, your reading should be done with the knowledge that a careful study of the story will reveal depths of meaning not available to the casual reader.

Knowledge of O'Connor's careful reading of Dante's *Divine Comedy* (an annotated edition exists in the O'Connor collection at Georgia College) and her extensive reading in Joseph Conrad and Henry James (in letters to friends, she confessed to reading most of the works of these two writers) can provide you with one way of getting into the story.

You might also wish to note that the story is built around several motifs (a conventional situation or incident employed in folklore, drama, or fiction) which have been part of the stock of writers since the beginning of recorded literature. The most obvious of these motifs include the "descent" or "initiation" story, the journey motif, and the contrast between the rural (good) and the urban (evil) environments.

Told from a generally omniscient point-of-view, the story opens with a picture of moonlight flooding the bedroom of Mr. Head and his grandson, Nelson. Seen in the dreamlike light of the moon, the room appears to be the domain of a very important person; the floorboards appear to be made of silver, the pillow ticking seems to be made of brocade, and the straight chair upon which Mr. Head has thrown his trousers seems to be an attentive servant awaiting the orders of a great man. The only dark spot in the room is the pallet upon which Nelson lies sleeping.

Within the first five paragraphs of the story, O'Connor is busy laying down a framework which will explain the details of the remainder of the story. Continuing with a modified omniscient narration, she combines the thoughts of Mr. Head (note that he is not called "Mr. Heart") concerning his moral mission for the coming day with authorial comments designed to lead the reader to the point which she ultimately wishes to make.

While you might reasonably expect to find Mr. Head viewing himself as especially qualified to teach Nelson about the world because "only with years does a man enter into the calm understanding of life that makes him a suitable guide for the young," you would hardly expect him, as a backwoods Georgian, to be familiar with the works of Dante or with the Apocryphal books of the Bible (those Old Testament books which are an integral part of the Catholic Bible but which are not considered to be a part of the Scriptures by many Protestants). By suggesting that Mr. Head is a Vergil "summoned in the middle of the night to go to Dante, or better, Raphael awakened by a blast of God's light to fly to the side of Tobias," O'Connor prepares the reader to draw parallels to two literary sources. The first of these is Dante's *Divine Comedy.* Vergil, a virtuous pagan, can lead Dante through Hell and Purgatory; but because he was never baptized, he is unable to lead Dante through Paradise. That task is reserved for Beatrice, a properly redeemed Christian. Raphael is an angel of God who is sent to guide Tobias (the name means "God is good") through a series of tasks which include freeing his future wife from the threat of a devil, and, more importantly, restoring the eyesight of his blind father. Although Mr. Head does help Nelson gain insight into the evils of the city, it is he, ironically, who benefits most from their experience. Raphael returns to Paradise after helping Tobias, but Mr. Head only returns to his *rural* Eden. This is, perhaps, O'Connor's way of suggesting that most men are *not* angels.

Mr. Head has awakened at two in the morning, and although his alarm clock does not work, he is not worried that he will fail to reawaken at four, so he goes back to sleep. A proud man, his confidence is based on a feeling that "sixty years had not dulled his responses; his physical reactions, like his moral ones were guided by his will and strong character." He is determined to get up before Nelson because the "boy was always irked when Mr. Head was the first up." Head's desire to arise before Nelson is a strong example of the multitude of petty conflicts which exist between these two people. Even the trip to town has been planned by Mr. Head in order to teach Nelson a lesson.

Although Mr. Head has been to Atlanta only three times in his life, he attempts to use his prior experiences to intimidate Nelson. Nelson was born in Atlanta, but despite the fact that he was left at age one with his grandfather, he insists that this trip will be his *second* trip to the city, "and I ain't but ten."

Nelson even suggests that his grandfather may not be able to find his way about, not having been to Atlanta in fifteen years. Mr. Head's response, "Have you ever . . . seen me lost?," leads Nelson (described as a child "never satisfied until he had given an impudent answer") to respond with, "It's nowhere around here to get lost at." This reference to being lost will take on new meaning at the end of the story when Mr. Head admits that he is indeed lost – not only in a physical sense but in a spiritual sense also.

Much of the conflict between these two characters arises because they are so much like one another. In fact, O'Connor may well have intended Nelson to function as a Doppelgänger in the story. If you have read Conrad's short story "The Secret Sharer," you may recall that Legatt, the murderer who is pulled from the sea by the Captain, functions as a Doppelgänger in that story (simply stated, a Doppelgänger is a character designed to act as a reflection of some aspect of the main character's personality or mind). In "The Artificial Nigger," Nelson's personality is a reflection of his grandfather's, and O'Connor is careful to point out this parallel at several places in the story. At one point, for example, she suggests that "they looked enough alike to be brothers and brothers not too far apart in age."

Mr. Head, awakened at 3:30 A.M. by the smell of frying fatback, rushes out to the kitchen to find Nelson already dressed and waiting on him. This "minor disaster," coupled with the image of Nelson in darkness at the beginning of the story, serves to function as a kind of foreshadowing which should signal the alert reader to suspect that Mr. Head's scheme to break Nelson's prideful nature may not be as successful as he had hoped. Attempting to save as much face as possible, Mr. Head tells Nelson, "It's no hurry. . . . You'll be there soon enough and it's no guarantee you'll like it when you do neither," because, as Mr. Head suggests, "It'll be full of niggers," a comment designed to undercut Nelson's self-confidence and to foreshadow the traumatic experiences which the two will undergo in the wicked city.

As they wait for the train to arrive, a "coarse-looking orange-colored sun" (orange, as a color symbol, is indicative of pride and ambition) begins to rise, slowly eclipsing the moon, by whose illusion-creating light Mr. Head was capable of seeing himself as Nelson's moral mentor. Mr. Head, plagued by thoughts that the train may not stop for them (thus causing him to lose face before Nelson), almost decides to return home when the train, "one yellow front light shining," stops for them. You may recall that the color yellow has been used by O'Connor to indicate betrayal in "The Life You Save May Be Your Own."

During the train ride to the city, Mr. Head is successful in intimidating Nelson, and O'Connor uses three distinct scenes to show us Mr. Head's success. The first scene involves Nelson's failure to recognize three blacks who walk through the car as "niggers." Nelson responds by suggesting that Mr. Head was the one really at fault for Nelson's not recognizing them as "niggers." "You said they were black. . . . You never said they were tan. How do you expect me to know anything when you don't tell me right?" Nelson, believing that the blacks purposely walked through the car to make a fool of him, feels that he can now understand "why his grandfather disliked them."

The second "learning" incident involves Mr. Head's confrontation with a black waiter in the dining car. Attempting to show Nelson the kitchen, Mr. Head is stopped by a black waiter, who announces that "Passengers are NOT allowed in the kitchen!" Mr. Head, "known at home for his quick wit," saves face by loudly responding that the reason for that rule was "the cockroaches would run the passengers out." Nelson, feeling a keen sense of pride in his grandfather, realizes that "he would be entirely alone in the world if he were ever lost from his grandfather."

Finally, when Nelson starts to leave the train at a suburban stop, Mr. Head prevents him from getting off. Even though Mr. Head has gained this knowledge because he himself made the same mistake during one of his trips to Atlanta and had to pay a man to take him on into the city, he does not tell Nelson this fact. Consequently, Nelson, "for the first time in his life . . . understood that his grandfather was indispensable to him."

You might also wish to note at this point that Mr. Head's apparent triumphs occur while the two are on the train. At the end of the story, O'Connor observes that the train, after having dropped off Nelson and Mr. Head, "disappeared like a frightened serpent into the woods." The traditional association of the serpent and Satan in Christian literature, coupled with the yellow light, may, on an anagogical level, indicate that O'Connor is using Mr. Head's *apparent* success at intimidating Nelson while on the train; she may also be suggesting that the serpent, "the craftiest of all the creatures the Lord God had made," works in mysterious ways even today.

Mr. Head's apparent victory as a "moral guide" begins to turn to ashes even as the two leave the train. Neither of them notices that they have left behind the paper sack containing their lunch, "some biscuits and a can of sardines" (loaves and fishes?).

Spit, as it were, from the train, just as Jonah was vomited forth from the belly of the whale, Mr. Head begins to lead Nelson through the city. Fearful of getting lost, he attempts to keep the train station always in sight; as a consequence, the two travel in a circle reminiscent of Vergil and Dante's journey through the Underworld.

As though O'Connor were deliberately attempting to create a parallel with the three scenes of Mr. Head's apparent victory on the train, she now shows Mr. Head suffering three very real defeats.

Walking the streets around the railway station, Nelson is impressed with the many stores (which they do not enter because Mr. Head got lost in one on his first trip to the city and doesn't want to repeat the experience). In addition, they use a weighing machine (a useless, mechanical, oracle-like "guide") which dispenses their incorrect weights and their "fortunes," and note that Nelson is directed by his card to "beware of dark women."

Finally Nelson is overcome by the glories of the city, and he proclaims, "This is where I come from!" Mr. Head is so appalled that Nelson likes the city that he shows him the entrance to the sewer system, describing it as an endless pitchblack tunnel into which a man might be sucked and never heard from again. Nelson "connected the sewer passages with the entrance to hell and understood for the first time how the world was put together in its lower parts." Nelson is momentarily shaken by this revelation, but he quickly recovers and comments, "You can always stay away from the holes." Mr. Head is unable to eradicate Nelson's enthusiasm for the city.

Mr. Head's second defeat occurs when Nelson notices they have been traveling in circles, and the boy accuses Mr. Head of not knowing where he is going. Determined to find some way of impressing Nelson with the evils of the city, Mr. Head loses sight of the train station, and they accidentally wander into a black neighborhood.

It is here that Nelson runs into the "dark woman" warned of on his fortune-telling card from the weighing machine. Chided by Mr. Head into asking for directions, Nelson approaches a large black woman in order to ask her how to get back to town. Paralyzed by the experience, Nelson "stood drinking in every detail of her," and "he felt as if he were reeling down through a pitchblack tunnel."

Some critics have suggested that Nelson's reaction to the mammoth maternity of the black woman before him was intended by O'Connor to depict a kind of prepubescent sexual awakening on Nelson's part. O'Connor, in a letter to a friend, notes that "I meant for her in an almost physical way to suggest the mystery of existence to him—he not only has never seen a nigger but he didn't know any women and I felt that such a black mountain of maternity would give him the required shock to start those black forms moving up from his subconscious."

When Nelson is pulled away from her by Mr. Head, who is embarrassed by Nelson's conduct, a sense of foreboding overcomes him, and he takes hold "of the old man's hand, a sign of dependence that he seldom showed." Because Mr. Head is so concerned with the shame of Nelson's conduct, he does not notice this change in Nelson's attitude. This failure to recognize the change in Nelson leads Mr. Head to commit one last error and to suffer another humiliating defeat.

When the two arrive at the trolley tracks to which the black woman directed them, Mr. Head follows the tracks in the wrong direction. Because Nelson, recovered from his experience with the black woman, has again begun to act sassy toward Mr. Head, Mr. Head decides that he must really teach the boy a lesson.

They finally arrive in a white neighborhood, and Nelson, exhausted by the heat and the long walk, collapses in a heap and falls asleep. Convinced that it is "sometimes necessary to teach a child a lesson he won't forget," Mr. Head conceals himself in an alley and waits for Nelson to wake up. But fearing that Nelson will not awaken in time to catch the train home, Mr. Head kicks a trash can, and the noise awakens Nelson. Frightened because he cannot see his grandfather, Nelson begins to run madly down the street with his grandfather in pursuit.

Mr. Head finally catches up to Nelson, just as the boy knocks down an elderly lady carrying groceries, and he also goes sprawling onto the pavement. Frightened by the woman's cry for a policeman and finally spotting his grandfather, Nelson "caught him around the hips and clung panting against him." Mr. Head senses what he thinks is the approach of a policeman behind him, and it is precisely at this moment that he commits his greatest sin against the boy. He denies him – "I never seen him before" – at which point "Nelson's fingers fell out of his [grandfather's] flesh."

Shocked and "repulsed by a man who would deny his own image," the crowd falls back, and Mr. Head passes through, seeing nothing before him but "a hollow tunnel that had once been a street." By denying his own flesh, Mr. Head has aligned himself with the sin of the Apostle Peter, who denied knowing Christ. With his third and final defeat, Mr. Head's pride – and not Nelson's pride – is shattered, and he experiences the pangs of guilt.

Walking aimlessly onward, Mr. Head tries to think of some way to soothe the injured Nelson, knowing "the boy was not of a forgiving nature." In desperation, he offers Nelson that most sovereign of all Georgia-patented elixers, a "Co' Cola," only to have the boy turn and stand with his back to him. Convinced that he will be beaten and robbed if they miss the train, Mr. Head feels that such a fate would justifiably be his "but he could not stand to think that his sins would be visited upon Nelson." Moving deeper into the depths of despair, Mr. Head finally feels that "if he saw a sewer entrance he would drop down into it and let himself be carried way."

Startled from his despair by the sound of two barking dogs, Mr. Head sees a man approaching and cries out to him, "I'm lost!" He ends his appeal with the unconscious prayer, "Oh Gawd I'm lost! Oh hep me Gawd I'm lost!" With this admission and appeal for help, Mr. Head's pride has clearly been shattered. He is completely humbled, and he has now, from O'Connor's point of view, reached the moment when he can benefit from God's offer of grace. This moment comes as the two walk toward the suburban station to which the man directed them, and it comes in a truly unexpected way.

Still distressed because Nelson has shown no signs of forgiving him, Mr. Head feels no joy in the prospect of returning home. Then his attention is captured by a battered and paint-chipped lawn ornament, "an artificial nigger."

In a letter to a friend, O'Connor comments, "What I had in mind to suggest with the artificial nigger was the redemptive quality of the Negro's suffering for us all." As described in the story, it seems as though Mr. Head and Nelson almost melt into one another's forms – "Mr. Head looked like an ancient child and Nelson like a miniature old man." They stand looking at the statue "as if they were faced with some great mystery, some monument to another's victory that brought them together in their common defeat." As Mr. Head recognizes the action of mercy on Nelson and on himself, he also recognizes that Nelson needs him to say something "to show that he was still wise." Although his trite comment, "They ain't got enough real ones here. They got to have an artificial one," is not the lofty statement he wishes to make, it is sufficient, and Nelson's hatred dissolves, indicated by his suggestion that they return home before they get lost again.

After they return to the clearing near their house, the moonlight imagery reappears, and they find themselves in a clearing with the treetops "fencing the junction like the protecting walls of a garden" (a return to the rural and almost Eden-like environment, free of the evils of the city). Mr. Head now sees things in a new light. No longer does he see his world as marred by a small dark spot (Nelson, sleeping in the shadows); he now sees that his silver, moonlight-lined world contains dark "clinkers" which glisten "with a fresh black light" (clinkers are the residue that remains when the "useful part" of coal has been burned).

Mr. Head's experience before the artificial nigger has humbled him – "Mr. Head had never known before what mercy felt like because he had been too good to deserve any, but he felt he knew now" – and he is now capable of seeing that he, too, is composed of a "useful part" of something, as well as "clinkers."

In the next-to-last paragraph of the story, O'Connor provides a description of the effect of the action of grace on Mr. Head. Such a complete explanation is unique in O'Connor's fiction; for that reason, you should be aware that from her point of view the action of grace should produce a similar degree of awareness in the hearts and minds of all her characters who choose to receive this gift from God.

The story ends, then, with the two characters safe in their rural haven. The journey into the wicked city completed, they have both brought back new and useful knowledge. Nelson, as Mr. Head had hoped, no longer sees the place of his birth as something to be overly proud of. He announces, "I'm glad I've went once, but I'll never go back again!" It is Mr. Head, however, who comes back with the greatest knowledge. He has learned that although all men are sinners (having inherited Adam's Original Sin), they are also capable of being redeemed by God's gift of grace.

GOOD COUNTRY PEOPLE

Hulga Hopewell of "Good Country People" is a unique character in O'Connor's fictional world. Although O'Connor uses the intellectual, or the pseudo-intellectual, in one of her novels and in seven of her short stories, Hulga is the only female in the bunch. Her gender, however, does not keep her from suffering the common fate of all the other O'Connor intellectuals. In every instance, the intellectual comes to realize that his belief in his ability to control his life totally, as well as control those things which influence it, is a faulty belief.

This story is divided into four rather distinct sections which help emphasize the relationships between the four central characters. By dividing the story into four loosely distinct sections, O'Connor is able to establish subtle *parallels* between the characters of Mrs. Freeman and Manley Pointer (a traveling Bible salesman) and between Mrs. Hopewell and her daughter, Hulga, while at the same time providing details which appear to emphasize the *different facets* of the four individual characters.

For example, O'Connor uses the day of Hulga's "enlightenment" in order to create parallels between Mrs. Freeman and Manley Pointer, while the flashbacks to the events of the previous day establish the parallels which exist between Hulga and her mother.

You might also wish to note that O'Connor's selection of names for her characters helps to establish their significance in the story. For example, the name "Hopewell" (hope well) characterizes both the mother and her daughter. Both women are individuals who simplistically believe that what is wanted can be had – although each of them is, in her own way, blind to the world as it really exists. Both women fail to see that the world (because it is a fallen world) is a mixture of good *and* evil. This misperception leads them to assume that the world is much simpler than it actually is.

Because both Hulga and her mother have accepted this false view of reality, each of them "hopes well" to tailor that world to meet her own needs – Mrs. Hopewell by living in a world where cliches operate as truth, and Hulga by insisting that there is nothing behind, or beyond, the surface world.

Although Mrs. Freeman (free man) is given a clearer view of the realities of the world (she does not, for example, accept either Hulga or Manley Pointer at face value), she chooses to concentrate on the diseased and the grotesque aspects of life.

The name Pointer (manly), not his real name, functions as a semi-obscene pun on one level, and it comes to point out, on another level, the depths to which humanity might descend if it follows only its "manly" nature.

In order to allow the reader to develop a degree of genuine sympathy for Hulga, O'Connor places her in an environment which would appall any sensitive person. Hulga is in constant contact with a vain but simple-minded mother and an apparently simple-minded but shrewd hired woman. Mrs. Hopewell survives in a self-made world of illusion, isolating herself from the real world by mouthing pseudo-philosophical, cliched maxims which only isolate her further from her daughter who has a Ph.D. in philosophy.

Included in Mrs. Hopewell's repertoire of "good country" philosophy are such old standards as "You're the wheel behind the wheel," "It takes all kinds to make the world," and "Everybody is different." But, significantly, Mrs. Hopewell cannot reconcile herself to a daughter who is "different," despite the fact that Mrs. Hopewell can sound as though she has an all-accepting, catholic compassion. In fact, Mrs. Hopewell would probably sum up her inability to understand her daughter-with-a-Ph.D. by saying, "She's brilliant but she doesn't have a grain of sense." Consequently, Mrs. Hopewell considers Hulga's acts of rebellion to be little more than pranks of an immature mind.

It is precisely Hulga's Ph.D. degree in philosophy which creates a major problem between the two women. Mrs. Hopewell thinks that girls should go to school and have a good time – but Hulga has attained the ultimate educational degree, and yet education did not "bring her out"; privately, Mrs. Hopewell is glad that there is "no more excuse for [Hulga] to go to school again." Mrs. Hopewell would like to brag about her daughter, as she can brag about Mrs. Freeman's daughters, but bragging about Hulga is next to impossible. Mrs. Hopewell can't say, "My daughter is a philosopher." That statement, as Mrs. Hopewell knows, is something that "ended with the Greeks and Romans."

Hulga's manner of dress also contributes to the vast misunderstanding that exists between the two women. Mrs. Hopewell thinks that Hulga's wearing "a six-year-old skirt and a yellow sweat shirt with a faded cowboy on a horse embossed on it" is idiotic, proof that despite Hulga's Ph.D. and her name change, she is "still a child."

In addition to Hulga's wearing inappropriate clothes, her name change (from "Joy" to "Hulga") cut such a wound into Mrs. Hopewell that she will never entirely heal. To change one's name from "Joy" to "Hulga," according to Mrs. Hopewell, was an act of ridiculously immature rebellion. Mrs. Hopewell is convinced that Joy pondered until she "hit upon the ugliest name in any language," and then legally changed her name.

Mrs. Hopewell is embarrassed and angry about her daughter's behavior, but she knows that she must ultimately accept it – because of the hunting *accident* which cost Joy her leg when she was ten. This misfortune is compounded by a doctor's opinion that Hulga will not live past forty because of a heart condition; furthermore, Hulga has been deprived of ever dancing and having what Mrs. Hopewell calls a "normal good time."

The chasm between the two women is even further deepened by Mrs. Hopewell's attitude toward the Freeman girls – as opposed to her attitude toward Hulga. Mrs. Hopewell likes to praise Glynese and Carramae by telling people that they are "two of the finest girls" she knows, and she also praises their mother, Mrs. Freeman, as a lady whom "she was never ashamed to take . . . anywhere or introduce . . . to anyone." In contrast, Mrs. Hopewell is deeply ashamed of Hulga's name, the way she dresses, and her behavior.

Hulga's own attitude toward the two Freeman girls is one of repulsion. She calls them "Glycerin" and "Caramel" (oily and sticky sweet). Mrs. Hopewell is aware that Hulga disapproves of the Freeman girls, but she herself remains enchanted by them, totally unconscious of her own daughter's deep need to be accepted – even though Hulga states that "If you want me, here I am – LIKE I AM."

As a result of Mrs. Hopewell's failure to understand Hulga, Hulga withdraws; she decides not to attempt any meaningful relationship with her mother. We see this withdrawal particularly in a scene in which her mother has just uttered a series of her favorite, ever-ready platitudes, and O'Connor focuses on Hulga's eyes. Hulga's eyes, she says, are "icy blue, with the look of someone who has achieved blindness by an act of will and means to keep it."

Hulga, then, by O'Connor's admission is "blind," and ironically, it is during one of Hulga's exchanges with her mother, while Hulga is attempting to reveal her mother's blindness to her (her lack of awareness) that Hulga fails; instead, she reveals a vast weakness in her own professedly atheistic views, laying her open later to Manley Pointer's attack.

Mrs. Hopewell had told Hulga, in simple, "good country" terms, that a smile on her face would improve matters ("a smile never hurt anything"). In a moment of seemingly immense insight, Hulga lashed out at her mother, yelling, "We are not our own light!" In addition, she cited a seventeenth-century Catholic philosopher, Malebranche, for uttering this truth initially.

O'Connor is showing us here that Hulga, with her Ph.D. degree in philosophy, has until now professed absolute atheism. To Hulga, there is no god and there is no afterlife; man is all. Now, however, we see that Hulga unconsciously *wants* to believe that there is a power greater than herself. Subconsciously, she deeply desires something to which she might surrender herself, as she later does to Pointer's advances. Thus, ironically, in pointing out her mother's "blindness," Hulga has revealed to us that she herself is blind about her own desires and her own view of reality.

Remember that until this moment, Hulga has subscribed to an atheistic viewpoint. She has believed that she was an iron-willed rationalist, as indicated by the underlined passage in one of her books that Mrs. Hopewell attempted to read. Hulga's conscious assumption that there was nothing behind the surface reality which we see around us is a far cry from the "truth" that she now cites in Malebranche's philosophy. Malebranche, a seventeenth-century Catholic philosopher, believed that even the simplest of bodily movements was possible only because of the supernatural power that was constantly present. This supernatural power metaphorically functioned as the strings between the puppet master (the mind) and the puppet (the body).

The ever-present hostility which exists between Hulga and her mother is undoubtedly aggravated by the presence of Mrs. Freeman, whom Hulga's mother idealizes as an example of "good country people." Hulga's mother naively believes in the absolute goodness of "good country people"; she believes that if a person can hire good country people, "you had better hang onto them." O'Connor, however, does not depict Mrs. Freeman as an example of "good country people."

On the contrary, Mrs. Freeman is depicted as a fairly shrewd woman who is capable of "using" Mrs. Hopewell's blindness to reality, just as Manley Pointer will later "use" Hulga's blindness to reality for his own selfish advantage. In fact, Mrs. Hopewell is so blind to reality that she believes that she can "use" Mrs. Freeman. She has heard that Mrs. Freeman always wants to "be into everything"; that being the case, Mrs. Hopewell believes that she can counter this character defect by putting Mrs. Freeman "in charge." We know, of course, that Mrs. Freeman is no fool when it comes to manipulating.

O'Connor further reinforces her view of Mrs. Freeman as a manipulator of Mrs. Hopewell by giving her, Mrs. Freeman, attributes which parallel those of Manley Pointer. For instance, both Mrs. Freeman and Manley Pointer are seen as "good country people" by Mrs. Hopewell; both have a morbid interest in Hulga's wooden leg; both of them allow their "victims" to form an erroneous view of "good country people"; and finally, both Pointer and Mrs. Freeman are described as having steely eyes capable of penetrating Hulga's facade.

The arrival of nineteen-year-old Manley Pointer, Bible salesman and con artist, is presented in highly realistic terms by O'Connor. He is familiar with all the slick tricks used by the typical door-to-door salesman, and he also has a second sense which enables him to take advantage of Mrs. Hopewell, even though she is not interested in entertaining a salesman of any description. His comment, "People don't like to fool with country people like me," touches a hidden switch in Mrs. Hopewell, and she responds with a barrage of platitudes concerning good country people and the world's lack of sufficient numbers of that breed. To her, "good country people are the salt of the earth." Asking to be excused for a moment, Mrs. Hopewell goes into the kitchen to check on dinner, where she is met by Hulga, who suggests that her mother "get rid of the salt of the earth . . . and let's eat."

When Mrs. Hopewell returns to the parlor, she finds Pointer with a Bible on each knee. As she attempts to get away from him, he mentions that he is just a poor country boy with a heart condition. This mention of a heart disease, paralleling Hulga's heart trouble, has a marked effect on Mrs. Hopewell, and she invites him to stay for dinner even though she is "sorry the instant she heard herself say it." Throughout the dinner, Pointer stares at Hulga, who eats rapidly, clears the table, and leaves the room.

As young Pointer is leaving, he arranges to meet Hulga the following day, and the banal conversation between the two of them clearly illustrates Hulga's naivete. She convinces herself that "events of significance" with "profound implications" have occurred. That night, she lies in bed imagining dialogues between herself and Pointer that are insane on the surface but which reach below to depths that no Bible salesman would be aware of. "Their conversation . . . had been of that kind," she says. She also imagines that she has seduced him and will have to deal with his remorse. She also imagines that she takes his remorse and changes it into a deeper understanding of life. Finally, Hulga imagines that she takes away all of Pointer's shame and turns it into "something useful."

When Hulga meets Pointer at the gate, she finds it easy to continue her misconceptions about his innocence and her wisdom. Their kiss – Hulga's first – is used by O'Connor to indicate that Hulga's plan may not go as smoothly as she imagines. Even though the kiss causes an extra surge of adrenalin, like that which "enables one to carry a packed trunk out of a burning house," Hulga is now convinced that nothing exceptional happened and that everything is "a matter of the mind's control."

Hulga, however, is wrong, and even O'Connor's color imagery which is inserted as Hulga and Pointer make their way to the old barn (likened at one point to a train which they fear may "slide away") contributes to the impression that Hulga may have met her match. The pink weeds and "speckled pink hillsides" (pink being the color symbolic of sensuality and the emotions) serve to emphasize how Hulga is slowly losing control of the situation.

Having reached the barn, the two climb into the loft, where Pointer actively begins to take control. Because Hulga's glasses interfere with their kissing, Pointer removes them and puts them in his pocket. The loss of Hulga's glasses symbolically marks her total loss of perception, and she begins to return his kisses, "kissing him again and again as if she were trying to draw all the breath out of him." Although Hulga tries to continue her "indoctrination" of the youth by explaining that she is "one of those people who have seen through to nothing," Pointer ignores her comments and continues to woo her, kissing her passionately and insisting that she tell him that she loves him. Finally, Hulga utters, "Yes, yes," and Pointer then insists that she prove it. This request leads Hulga to believe that she has "seduced him without even making up her mind to try."

Hulga is outraged to discover that the "proof of love" demanded by Pointer is that she show him where her wooden leg joins her body; Hulga is "as sensitive about her artificial leg as a peacock is about his tail." No one ever touches it but her. She takes care of it as someone else might take care of his soul.

In an address delivered before a Southern Writers Conference, O'Connor commented on the wooden leg: "We're presented with the fact that the Ph.D. is spiritually as well as physically crippled . . . and we perceive that there is a wooden part of her soul that corresponds to her wooden leg." Since this is the case, it is not surprising that Pointer's comment that it is her leg which "makes her different" produces the total collapse of Hulga's plan.

O'Connor's account of Hulga's reaction is worth examining in detail since it stresses the fact that Hulga's decision to surrender the leg is essentially an *intellectual* one:

> She sat staring at him. There was nothing about her
> face or her round freezing-blue eyes to indicate that this
> had moved her; but she felt as if her heart had stopped
> and left her mind to pump her blood. She decided that
> for the first time in her life she was face to face with
> real innocence. This boy, with an instinct that came from
> beyond wisdom, had touched the truth about her. When
> after a minute, she said in a hoarse high voice, "All right,"
> it was like surrendering to him completely. It was like
> losing her own life and finding it again, miraculously in
> his.

O'Connor's selection of a well-known biblical parallel ("He who finds his life will lose it, and he who loses his life for my sake will find it," Matthew 10:39) clearly depicts Hulga's rational surrender to Pointer and firmly underlines the significance of her rational decision within the context of the story.

Having made her commitment to Pointer, Hulga allows herself to indulge in a fantasy in which "she would run away with him and that every night he would take the leg off and every morning put it back on again." Since she has surrendered her leg (now functioning emblematically as her soul) to Pointer, Hulga feels "entirely dependent on him."

Hulga's epiphany, or moment of grace, occurs as a result of

Pointer's betrayal of her faith in him and his destruction of her intellectual pretensions. Prior to his betrayal of her, Hulga considered herself to be the intellectual superior of all those around her. She relied upon the wisdom of this world to guide her, contrary to the biblical warning to "See to it that no one deceives you by philosophy and vain deceit, according to human traditions, according to the elements of the world and not according to Christ" (Colossians 2:8).

However, in order for Hulga to progress beyond her present state, it is necessary for her to realize that "God turned to foolishness the 'wisdom' of this world" (I Corinthians 1:20). From Hulga's point of view, the surrender of her leg was an intellectual decision; consequently, the destruction of her faith in the power of her own intellect can come only through betrayal by the one whom she rationally decided to believe in, to have faith in.

Manley Pointer plays his role by removing Hulga's leg and setting it out of her reach. When she asks that he return it, he refuses, and from a hollowed-out Bible (emblematic perhaps of his own religious condition), he produces whiskey, prophylactics, and playing cards with pornographic pictures on them. When a shocked Hulga asks whether or not he is "good country people," as he claims he is, Pointer replies, "Yeah . . . but it ain't held me back none. I'm as good as you any day in the week."

Disillusioned, Hulga tries to reach her wooden leg (soul) only to have Pointer easily push her down. Physically defeated, Hulga attempts to use her intellect to shame Pointer into returning the leg. She hisses, "You're a fine Christian! You're just like them all – say one thing and do another," only to hear Pointer tell her that he is *not* a Christian. As Pointer is leaving the barn loft with Hulga's wooden leg, he further disillusions Hulga by telling her that he has obtained a number of interesting things from other people, including a glass eye, in the same way that he took Hulga's leg.

Pointer's final comment strips Hulga of her last resource – her feeling of intellectual superiority. "And I'll tell you another thing," Pointer says, "You ain't so smart. I been believing in nothing ever since I was born."

Consequently, it is a totally chastened Hulga who turns "her churning face toward the opening" and watches Pointer disappear, a "blue figure struggling successfully over the green speckled lake." The color imagery associated with Pointer as he leaves (blue, with heaven and heavenly love; green, with charity and regeneration of the soul), coupled with the image of walking on the water, would appear to indicate that O'Connor wishes the reader to see Pointer as an instrument of God's grace for Hulga. Although Pointer may seem an unlikely candidate for the role of grace bringer, O'Connor, in commenting on the action of grace in her stories, has noted that "frequently it is an action in which the devil has been the unwilling instrument of grace."

O'Connor uses the final paragraphs of the story to make clear the parallel which she established earlier between Hulga and her mother. Hulga has now undergone mortification, and Mrs. Hopewell appears to be facing a future revelation. Mrs. Hopewell's analysis of Pointer, "He was so simple . . . but I guess the world would be better off if we were all that simple," is as wrong as Hulga's earlier assessment of Pointer. The final irony in the story involves Mrs. Freeman's response: "Some can't be that simple . . . I know I never could." Thus, the reader is left with the impression that Mrs. Hopewell will also have to undergo an epiphanal experience which will destroy the confidence she has in her ability to control and to use Mrs. Freeman.

EVERYTHING THAT RISES MUST CONVERGE

On the surface,"Everything That Rises Must Converge" appears
to be a simple story. Finally, it seems, O'Connor has written a story
which we can easily read and understand without having to struggle
with abstract religious symbolism. Mrs. Chestny is a bigot who feels
that blacks should rise, "but on their own side of the fence." Because
she condescendingly offers a new penny to a small black child, she
is, from the point of view of her son, Julian, punished with the much
deserved humiliation of being struck by the child's mountainous black
mother. It is Julian who recognizes that the black woman who hits
Mrs. Chestny with her purse represents "the whole colored race which
will no longer take your condescending pennies." It is he who also
recognizes that "the old manners are obsolete" and that his mother's
"graciousness is not worth a damn." It is he (as well as we) who begins
to realize, as we watch his mother die from the blow, that the world
is, perhaps, not that simple. It is *not* a world in which everything is
either black or white. Thus, we realize that "Everything That Rises
Must Converge" is not entirely a "simple story."

Yet, the basic plot of the story appears to be very simple. One
evening, following the racial integration of the public buses in the
South, Julian Chestny is accompanying his mother to an exercise class
at the "Y." During the ride downtown, they talk to several people on
the bus. Then a black woman boards the bus wearing a hat which
is identical to the hat worn by Mrs. Chestny. Mrs. Chestny begins
a conversation with the small child of that black woman, and when
they get off of the bus together, Mrs. Chestny offers the small black
boy a shiny penny. The black woman, insulted by Mrs. Chestny's gift
to the child, strikes her with a big purse, knocking her to the ground.
Julian, who feels his mother has been taught a good lesson, begins
to talk to her about the emergence of blacks in the new South. While
he is speaking to his mother, she suffers a stroke (or a heart attack)
as a result of the blow, and she dies, leaving Julian grief-stricken and
running for help.

As we noted, the plot line of the story appears to be simple; the major impact of the story, however, is generated by the interaction of the attitudes held by Julian and his mother. Their conflicting viewpoints are designed to highlight a conflict between generations, on the one hand, and, on the other hand, they provide a situation which O'Connor can use to make a comment on what she considers to be the proper basis for all human relationships—not just black/white relationships.

To enter this story, which was first published in 1961, it is necessary to recall the social upheaval which the nation in general and the South in particular was experiencing during the 1950s. Black Americans, long treated as second-class citizens, began to make themselves heard in America by demanding that they be given equal rights under the law. In 1954, the Supreme Court ruled that segregation by color in public buses was unconstitutional, and the protest movement gained force. Accounts of bus boycotts and freedom marches were part of the daily news reports, and Southern writers were expected to give their views on "relations between people in the South, especially between Negroes and whites."

O'Connor gave answers to those questions in two interviews granted in 1963, two years after this story appeared and one year before her death. Her views do much to illuminate the anagogical level of the story itself. From O'Connor's point of view, a society divided about fifty-fifty requires "considerable grace for the two races to live together." The existence of what she called "a code of manners" had made it possible for them to live together. She stated that "the South has survived in the past because its manners, however lopsided or inadequate they might have been, provided enough social discipline to hold us together and give us an identity."

While admitting that those old manners were obsolete, she maintained that "the new manners will have to be based on what was best in the old ones—in their real basis of charity and necessity." She also suggested that while the rest of the country believed that granting blacks their rights would settle the racial problem, "the South has to evolve a way of life in which the two races can live together in mutual forbearance." For this, "You don't form a committee . . . or pass a resolution; both races have to work it out the hard way."

In an interview which appeared a month later, when she was asked about Southern manners, O'Connor noted that "manners are the next best thing to Christian charity. I don't know how much pure unadulterated Christian charity can be mustered in the South, but I have confidence that the manners of both races will show through in the long run." Finally, in a letter written to a friend on September 1, 1963, she observed that topical writing is poison but, she said, "I got away with it in 'Everything That Rises' but only because I say a plague on everybody's house as far as the race business goes."

The title of this story and of O'Connor's second collection of stories is taken from the works of Pierre Teilhard de Chardin, a priest-paleontologist. O'Connor reviewed and was impressed by several of his works and, at one stage in her life, she appears to have been interested in Teilhard's attempt to integrate religion and science. Most simply stated, Teilhard speculated that the evolutionary process was producing a higher and higher level of consciousness and that ultimately that consciousness, now become spiritual, would be complete when it merged with the Divine Consciousness at the Omega point. At that time, God would become "all in all." In *The Phenomenon of Man*, Teilhard argues that "the goal of ourselves" is not to be found in our individuality but in the surrender of our ego to the Divine. "The true ego grows in inverse proportion to 'egotism'." We can, he argues, "only find our person by uniting together."

As you work with this story, it is important to notice O'Connor's use of point-of-view. By using a modified omniscient point-of-view, she is able to move unobtrusively from reporting the story as an outside observer to reporting events as they are reflected through Julian's consciousness. The most obvious scenes in which she uses the latter technique are introduced by the comment that "Julian was withdrawing into the inner compartment of his mind where he spent most of his time" and by the comment that "he retired again into the high-ceilinged room." These scenes close with the comments "The bus stopped . . . and shook him from his meditation," and "He was tilted out of his fantasy again as the bus stopped." Although other sections of the story are not so clearly marked, you should note that you are generally given Julian's reaction to things with the author intruding only when it becomes necessary to show external, physical events, or to make a specific comment.

Because we see the events in the story primarily from Julian's point-of-view, it is easy for us to misjudge the character of his mother. As a native of the Old South, she carries with her attitudes which we now recognize as wrong-headed or prejudicial. Her comments that

"They [the blacks] should rise, yes, but on their own side of the fence," and "The ones I feel sorry for . . . are the ones that are half white," mark her indelibly as a member of that generation which failed to concern itself with the problem of social justice. Her uneasiness at riding on an integrated bus is illustrated by her comment, "I see we have the bus to ourselves," and by her observation, "The world is in a mess everywhere . . . I don't know how we've let it get in this fix." These comments reveal her to be an individual who will be slow to change her attitudes (if they can be changed at all) and as an individual who has a nostalgic sense of longing for past traditions.

To assume that such attitudes always conceal a hatred for blacks is an error into which many unthinking liberals fall. Anyone who has ever read Faulkner's funeral oration on the death of Caroline Barr, the black servant of the Faulkner family (she became the model for Dilsey in *The Sound and the Fury*) should realize that to recognize a social distinction is *not* to feel hatred or disrespect for a person who is not in the same social class as ourselves. Certainly, the Apostle Paul makes no such assumptions when he writes of the relationship between slaves and masters in the sixth chapter of Ephesians. He begins by commanding, "Slaves, obey your human masters. . . . Do your work as slaves cheerfully, then, as though you served the Lord, and not merely men," and he concludes by cautioning the masters to treat their slaves well because "you and your slaves belong to the same Master in heaven, who treats everyone alike."

Because Julian interprets his mother's comment concerning her feelings for Caroline, her black nurse, as little more than a bigot's shibboleth, he is unable to understand her act of giving a penny to Carver, the small black boy in the story. In a simpler time – before sick individuals put pieces of razor blades or pins in the trick-or-treat candies and apples of the Halloween season – it was not at all uncommon for older people to carry treats for the kiddies they might meet. A stick of gum, a piece of candy, a new penny – these were things that would give a child pleasure, and things that would give the older person a sense of continuity with the new generation. These were gifts of affection, not condescension. In a society where man is fragmented from his fellow man, however, such gifts have come to be suspect – temptations to perversion, acts of condescension, or, at the very least, attempts by old busybodies trying to stick their noses where they are not wanted.

To see Mrs. Chestny as a simple bigot is to ignore the clues to her character which O'Connor gives us. As we examine these clues, we will find that Mrs. Chestny resembles another of O'Connor's characters, the grandmother from "A Good Man Is Hard to Find." In a series of comments prefacing a reading of that story, O'Connor noted that one of the teachers who had attempted to depict the grandmother of the story as evil was surprised to find that his students resisted that evaluation of her. O'Connor notes, "I had to tell him that they resisted it because they all had grandmothers or great-aunts just like her at home, and they knew from personal experience that the old lady lacked comprehension, but that she had a good heart."

Numerous clues appear to reinforce this view of Mrs. Chestny. She is described as having "sky-blue" eyes (blue, you may remember, often symbolizes heaven and heavenly love in Christian symbology); Mrs. Chestny's eyes, O'Connor says, were "as innocent and untouched by experience as they must have been when she was ten." She is repeatedly described as being child-like: "She might have been a little girl that he had to take to town"; her feet "dangled like a child's and did not quite reach the floor"; and Julian sees her as "a particularly obnoxious child in his charge."

Mrs. Chestny is also depicted as one who "finds her person by uniting together," according to one of Teilhard's concepts. She was a widow but she had "struggled fiercely" to put Julian through school, and at the time of the story, she is still supporting him. "Her teeth had gone unfilled so that his could be straightened," and she even offers to take off her hideous hat when she thinks that it might be the cause of his irritated, "grief-stricken" face.

In addition, she reaches out to those around her on the bus by engaging them in conversation, even if that conversation is inane and naive. It is also this quality of her personality that allows her to forget that the black woman has an identical hat and to turn her attention to Carver, the black woman's child. Her fascination with the small boy and her ability to play with him indicate that they, at least, have risen above strict self-interest and have "converged" in a momentary Christian love for one another. It is this act, more than anything else, that gives the lie to Julian's contention that true culture "is in the mind," and places it, as Mrs. Chestny argues, "in the heart."

Julian lacks all respect for his mother and does not hide his lack of respect. This lack of respect is shown by his thinking of himself as a martyr because he takes her to her reducing class, by his making fun of her new hat, by his desire to slap her and by his "evil urge to break her spirit." He sees everything in terms of his own "individuality." It is he who takes what Teilhard describes as "the dangerous course of seeking fulfillment in isolation." We are told that he likes to spend most of his time by withdrawing into a kind of mental bubble, especially when things around him are a bother, and in that bubble, "he was safe from any kind of penetration from without." Within that bubble, he creates an image of himself and the world around him. These are images, however, which have absolutely no validity.

O'Connor arranges the events in such a way that no one who reads the story should have any doubts about the character of Julian. Even though his mother remembers the old days and her grandfather's mansion which she used to visit, she can be content to live in a rather rundown neighborhood. Julian sees the neighborhood as ugly and undesirable and, in regard to his great-grandfather's mansion, he feels that it is he, not his mother, "who could have appreciated it." He condemns her for being a widow and is ungrateful for the sacrifices she has made for him. Most damaging of all is his feeling that he "had cut himself emotionally free of her."

Julian prides himself on his freedom from prejudice, but we discover that he is just fooling himself. He attempts to sit beside blacks and start conversations with them if they appear to be upper-class individuals. He dreams that he might teach his mother a lesson by making friends with "some distinguished Negro professor or lawyer." If she were ill, he might be able to find only a Negro doctor to treat her or—"the ultimate horror"—he might bring home a "beautiful suspiciously Negroid woman."

Ironically, his greatest successes are with a "distinguished-looking dark brown man" who turns out to be an undertaker and with a "Negro with a diamond ring on his finger" who turns out to be a seller of lottery tickets. When the militant black woman with the small boy, Carver, chooses to sit beside him rather than beside his mother, Julian is annoyed by her action.

Just as Julian tends to misunderstand his own motivations, he also misunderstands those of his mother. Observing the shocked look on her face as she sees the black woman sit beside him, Julian is convinced that it is caused by her recognition that "she and the woman had, in a sense, swapped sons." He is convinced that she will not realize the "symbolic significance of this," but that she would "feel it." The irony of this scene comes from the reader's realization that the two women have, indeed, changed sons. Mrs. Chestny and Carver are innocent and outgoing; they, therefore, are able to "converge" – to come together. Julian and Carver's mother, on the other hand, are both filled with hostility and anger; for them, there is not, nor can there ever be, any true convergence. The final irony in the scene comes when Julian realizes that the stunned look on his mother's face was caused by the presence of identical hats on the two women – not by the seating arrangements.

When Julian realizes that the hat is the cause of his mother's discomfort, he takes pleasure in watching her pained reaction, having only momentarily "an uncomfortable sense of her innocence." When he recognizes that his mother will be able to recover from this shock, he is dismayed because she has been taught no lesson.

Mrs. Chestny and Carver are drawn together because she finds all children "cute" and, we are told, "she thought little Negroes were on the whole cuter than little white children." Carver responds to Mrs. Chestny's affection by scrambling "onto the seat beside his love," much to the chagrin of both his mother and Julian. Carver's mother attempts to separate the two but is not totally successful as they play peek-a-boo games cross the aisle. Carver's mother is described as "bristling" and filled with "rage" because her son is attracted to Mrs. Chestny. She even threatens to "knock the living Jesus out of Carver" because he will not ignore the woman who has smiled at him, using a smile which, according to Julian's point of view, she used "when she was being particularly gracious to an inferior."

As the four people leave the bus, Julian has an "intuition" that his mother will try to give the child a nickel. "The gesture would be as natural to her as breathing." He even attempts to prevent the gesture, but is unsuccessful. His mother, unable to locate a nickel, attempts to give Carver a new penny. Carver's mother reacts violently to what she assumes to be a gesture of condescension. She stares, "her face frozen with frustrated rage," at Julian's mother, and then she "seemed to explode like a piece of machinery that had been given one ounce of pressure too much." She strikes Julian's mother to the ground with her mammoth red pocketbook, shouting, "He don't take nobody's pennies!"

That this action represents another act of convergence in the story is obvious. Carver's mother can afford the same hat as Julian's mother, and she can ride in the same section of the bus. The violence of this convergence, however, illustrates what can happen when the old "code of manners" governing relationships between whites and blacks has broken down. Julian's mother is living according to an obsolete code of manners and, consequently, she offends Carver's mother by her actions. Because Carver's mother is determined to exercise her legal rights, according to the letter of the law, she fails to exercise the "mutual forbearance" which O'Connor deems necessary to a successful resolution of racial tensions in the new South.

The final convergence in the story begins when Julian discovers that his mother is more seriously hurt than he had suspected. At first, he felt that she had been taught a good lesson by the black woman, and he attempted to impress upon her the changes which were taking place in the South. "Don't think that was just an uppity Negro woman. . . . That was the whole colored race who will no longer take your condescending pennies." It is only after Julian realizes that his mother may be seriously hurt that his own movement toward convergence takes place.

As Mrs. Chestny staggers away from Julian, calling for her grandfather and for Caroline, individuals with whom she had had a loving relationship, Julian feels her being swept away from him, and he calls for her, "Mother! . . . Darling, sweetheart, wait!" His attempt at convergence with his mother comes too late as she dies before him, one unseeing eye raking his face and finding nothing.

With the death of his mother, Julian is brought to the point where he will be unable to postpone for long the epiphany which will reveal to him the nature of evil within him. Although "the tide of darkness seemed to sweep him back to her, postponing from moment to moment his entry into the world of guilt and sorrow," he will soon come to know, as did Mr. Head, "that no sin was too monstrous for him to claim as his own." Having thus been made aware of his depravity, Julian will have been placed in a position which may produce repentance and ultimately redemption.

THE FINAL TRILOGY

In a 1959 interview with a writer for the *Atlanta Journal,* O'Connor told a reporter that she could wait for a larger audience for her fiction because "A few readers go a long way if they're the right kind." She went on to say, "You want, of course, to get what you want to show across to him, but whether he likes it or not is of no concern of the writer." The rigor of this statement may be accounted for by the fact that her health was better than it had been for some time and because she had just received a $10,000 grant from the Ford Foundation.

By 1964, however, O'Connor's health was beginning to fail, and by April of that year, as a result of an abdominal operation, the lupus was reactivated. By August she was dead. This loss of health may be one way to account for the marked change which occurs in her final three stories. In her earlier stories, the religious content, while unquestionably present, generally tends to be covert. Even in those stories where the religious element is most obvious, the reader is given an option which allows him to explain the events of the story on a purely secular basis. Harry, in "The River," can be seen as a young boy whose premature death is brought on by a group of religious freaks and fanatics. In a story called "The Enduring Chill," Asbury Fox's vision of the Holy Ghost descending upon him may be explained as a delusion brought on by the fever from which he is suffering. Only in "The Artificial Nigger," which O'Connor claimed to be her favorite story, can one find an unambiguously stated religious conclusion.

Consequently, the extremely overt use of religious themes in her final three stories comes as a shock to readers accustomed to the less obvious use of religious themes in her earlier stories. It is as though O'Connor, fearing that her position might be misunderstood or fearing, perhaps, that she could wait no longer, wishes to leave no doubt about her concerns and beliefs.

REVELATION

The first of the final three stories, "Revelation," concludes with a heavenly vision visited upon Mrs. Turpin, the protagonist of the story. Her major flaw, which is repeatedly revealed throughout the course of the story, is the great sense of satisfaction she takes in her own sense of propriety. Armed with this grand illusion, she self-righteously marches through life smiting the Philistines hip and thigh.

The first two-thirds of the story is set in the waiting room of a doctor's office where Mrs. Turpin has taken her husband, Claud, for treatment. It is here that she occupies her thoughts by placing the occupants of the waiting room into what she considers to be their "proper categories," using cliches which clearly reveal her view of the world in which she finds herself. She is aided in these activities because the waiting room is filled with people from several different social categories. Present are the "lady" and her daughter, Mary Grace, an acne-faced teenager who is reading a book entitled *Human Development*. Also present are an elderly gentleman, a mother and a child whom Mrs. Turpin considers "white trashy," an old woman, and a younger woman, "not white-trash, just common."

O'Connor exposes Mrs. Turpin's naive hypocrisy by recounting the conversation which takes place in the office and by revealing Mrs. Turpin's innermost thoughts. Mrs. Turpin lives by what O'Connor has called the "Southern code of manners." This code allows her to appear genteel on the surface and to keep to herself the less attractive thoughts which seethe behind her facade of gentility. We learn that she considers herself very fortunate because she sees herself and Claud as members of the class of "home-and-land owners." Above are people with more land, bigger houses, and money; below are the home-owners only, and at the bottom of the heap are the blacks and the white trash. With deft strokes, O'Connor outlines a complete milieu, laying bare both good and bad aspects of that society.

During the course of the conversation, Mrs. Turpin notes that Mary Grace, the Wellesley student, keeps looking at her as though she "knew her in some intense and personal way, beyond time and place and condition." Finally the girl, exasperated by the mannered politeness which has surrounded her, throws the *Human Development* book at Mrs. Turpin, striking her in the head. She then rushes across the room and begins to choke Mrs. Turpin. Finally, subdued and sedated, she replies to Mrs. Turpin's question, "What have you got to say to me?" She says, "Go back to hell where you came from, you old wart hog." This response strikes Mrs. Turpin with the force of another physical blow.

It is interesting to note that O'Connor, in a letter to a friend, identified herself with Mary Grace. One might speculate, on the basis of that identification, that O'Connor came to recognize the problems of a social attitude which, although not evil in and of itself, is capable of undercutting true Christian charity.

Mrs. Turpin returns home only to be plagued by Mary Grace's statement. Even her practice of bringing ice water to the black help and gaining their sympathy fails to restore her earlier sense of well-being. This is so because we know that her actions are based more on proper manners than on true charity; earlier, we heard her say, "I sure am tired of buttering up niggers, but you got to love em if you want em to work for you." The blacks, in their turn, retreat behind their own wall of manners, and they flatter Mrs. Turpin by threatening to "kill" Mary Grace for attacking her, by noting, "You the sweetest white lady I know," and by declaring, "Jesus satisfied with her." Mrs. Turpin is aware that the blacks are only using these statements to preserve their relationship with her and that they are not sincere. O'Connor noted, "The uneducated Southern Negro is not the clown he is made out to be. He's a man of very elaborate manners and great formality which he uses superbly for his own protection and to insure his own privacy." She goes on to say, "All this may not be ideal, but the Southerner has enough sense not to ask for the ideal but only for the possible, the workable." Mrs. Turpin's ability to recognize the insincerity of the blacks does not, however, help her to recognize that she is equally insincere in her dealings with them.

Still frustrated, Mrs. Turpin marches off to the pig parlor with the "look of a woman going single-handed, weaponless, into battle," where, in outright rebellion, she enters into a direct conflict with the Deity. In a letter to a friend, O'Connor notes, "I like Mrs. Turpin as well as Mary Grace. You got to be a very big woman to shout at the Lord across a hogpen. She's a country female Jacob." (The story of Jacob is recorded in the last twenty-five chapters of Genesis. The operative reference here is to Genesis 32:22–32, where Jacob wrestles with the angel and is told, "You shall no longer be called Jacob, but Israel, because you have contended with God and men, and have triumphed." Israel, then, becomes one of the important ancestors of the House of David, the line from which Christ descends.)

In her confrontation with God, Mrs. Turpin begins with the question, "Why me?" She then notes that even if He were to decide to "put that bottom rail on top. There'll still be a top and bottom!" Finally, she demands, "Who do you think you are?"

Mrs. Turpin's answer is presented through an epiphany which causes her to reevaluate her assumptions concerning her specific value in the divine scheme of things. You should note that her epiphanal moment is introduced by a change in nature and is supported by typical O'Connor color imagery. Also note that she gazes into the pig parlor "as if [she were looking] through the very heart of mystery" and that it is "as if she were absorbing some abysmal life-giving knowledge." Her tenacity is rewarded by a vision in which she sees "a vast horde of souls" marching into heaven. (O'Connor noted in the letter mentioned above that Mrs. Turpin's "vision is Purgatorial.") In that marching horde are "whole companies of white trash . . . bands of black niggers in white robes, and battalions of freaks and lunatics." It is only at the end of the procession that she sees people "who, like herself and Claud, had always had a little of everything and the God-given wit to use it right." She sees them "marching behind the others with great dignity, accountable as they had always been for good order and common sense and respectable behavior." You should remember that Mrs. Turpin has spent her life ranking individuals in what she takes to be "the proper order." While doing this, she has forgotten the clear teachings of Christ who said, "But many who are now first will be last, and many who are now last will be first" (Matthew 19:30). Consequently, she discovers "by their shocked and altered faces that even their virtues were being burned away."

The story ends with Mrs. Turpin walking back to the house. "In the woods around her the invisible cricket choruses had struck up, but what she heard were the voices of souls climbing upward into the starry field and shouting hallelujah." Although Mrs. Turpin's vision is not presented with the degree of high seriousness which usually accompanies the traditional presentation of a religious experience, there appears to be no question that O'Connor intends the reader to see Mrs. Turpin as one of the elect – saved, however mysteriously, by the grace of a forgiving God.

PARKER'S BACK

The overt religious message presented in "Revelation" is used again by O'Connor in "Parker's Back." This story was composed by O'Connor while she was lying in the hospital a few weeks before her death. The story has the salvation of a hard-drinking, woman-chasing heathen as its main theme.

The protagonist, O. E. Parker, resembles Hazel Motes, the protagonist of O'Connor's first novel, *Wise Blood*. Both characters undergo a disturbing experience at a fair, both try to reject any involvement with religion, and both finally succumb to the demands of the spirit. As you work with this story, pay particular attention to the chronology of the story. O'Connor does not follow a strict time sequence, but, instead, she uses flashbacks to provide background information.

Parker's initial awakening occurs at a fair where he sees a tattooed man whose "skin was patterned in . . . a single intricate design of brilliant color." This experience has a subtle effect on the fourteen-year-old boy, who prior to that time had never felt "there was anything out of the ordinary about the fact that he existed." After seeing the tattooed man, however, he becomes unsettled, and it is "as if a blind boy had been turned so gently in a different direction that he did not know that his direction had been changed."

Following this awakening, Parker tries to emulate the tattooed man by having himself tattooed also. Even though he discovers that his tattoos "were attractive to the kind of girls he liked but who had never liked him before," and that each new tattoo could temporarily ease the sense of dissatisfacion which he feels, he becomes frustrated because "he had not achieved that transforming unity of being that the intricately patterned skin of the tattooed man at the fair represented."

Following a five-year term in the navy, from which he was discharged for going a.w.o.l., Parker rents a shack in the country, purchases an old truck, and takes "various jobs which he kept as long as it suited him." While working at one of these jobs ("He was buying apples by the bushel and selling them for the same price by the pound to isolated homesteaders on back country roads"), Parker meets the hawk-eyed, horny-handed, sin-sniffing female who later becomes his wife. Although Parker acknowledges her uncommon ugliness, he finds himself repeatedly returning to court the woman who has rejected his tattoos as "a heap of vanity."

The courtship of Sarah (the name means "princess" or "mistress") Ruth ("friend" or "companion") Cates by O.E. Parker proceeds on the basis of his furnishing fruit for her entire family. At their third meeting, Sarah Ruth succeeds in coaxing Parker to reveal his full name on the condition that she will never reveal it to anyone. Parker's refusal to acknowledge his full name can be seen as his refusal to recognize that even he has a role to play in the divine scheme. Later, however, after he is touched by grace, he is then able to accept his full name.

The symbolic significance of names and name changes in O'Connor's works is one element of the stories which should not be overlooked. Traditionally, it marks the passage from adolescence to adulthood (Timmy becomes Timothy), emphasizes a change in one's view of himself or herself (Joy becomes Hulga), or it indicates a change in the status of an individual (Jacob, the scoundrel who cheats his brother Esau out of his birthright, becomes Israel, one of the ancestors of the House of David).

Parker's having revealed his full name to Sarah Ruth establishes a bond between the two which ultimately leads Parker to marry her even though he has no conscious desire to do so. After they are married, he sometimes suspects that "she had married him because she meant to save him." You should also note that, in addition to the meaning of her name, O'Connor also plants other suggestions which point out Sarah Ruth's function in the story. When Parker first meets her, she is described as "a giant, hawk-eyed angel." Also, he is driven to get a tattoo which will please her. And after he has that tattoo, he finds her "icepick eyes" are the only comfort he can "bring to mind."

Parker and Sarah Ruth are married, and Parker becomes progressively more dissatisfied with his life. His preoccupation with "a suitable design for his back" causes him to drive a broken-down tractor into the only tree in a field where he is baling hay. The tractor upsets and catches fire, and Parker finds himself in the presence of a metaphorical burning bush. The obvious parallel with Moses' experience is reinforced by O'Connor's comment that if "he had known how to cross himself he would have done so." As a result of this spiritual experience – which he interprets as only a sign that the tattoo on his back should be that of the face of God – Parker drives barefoot into the city and contacts a tattoo artist.

In addition to appreciating the wild humor with which Parker's adventures in the city are related, you should note that serious things are going on in this section of the story. Parker rejects all the romantic pictures of Christ as he flips through the book of available designs because he is convinced that when he reaches "the one ordained, a sign would come."

Finally, he is compelled to select a "Byzantine Christ with all-demanding eyes." Even though Parker is caught up in a rush of events which he cannot control, he still attempts to avoid the "someone" who is trailing him. That "someone" is, of course, the inexorable approach of the Divine which Parker has been trying to avoid. His experiences with the tattooist (he denies that he is "saved," and, initially, he refuses to look at the finished tattoo), his attempt to get drunk, his fighting with the men who ridicule his new tattoo, and his expulsion from the pool hall (described as being like "the ship from which Jonah had been cast into the sea") are all elements within the story which function to emphasize Parker's attempt to avoid acceptance of his new spiritual condition.

This lack of acceptance is carried still further, and although Parker now realizes that "the eyes that were now forever on his back were eyes to be obeyed," he makes one final attempt to return to his former state by returning to Sarah Ruth. He feels that she "would clear up the rest of it, and she would at least be pleased." As he drives homeward, "he observed that his dissatisfaction was gone, but he felt not quite like himself. It was as if he were himself but a stranger to himself, driving into a new country."

The change in Parker is in some way intuitively recognized by Sarah Ruth, who refuses to let him into the house when he arrives home. His insistence that "It's me, old O. E.," does not convince Sarah Ruth to let him in. O'Connor's use of the expression "old O. E.," is evidently designed to call attention to at least three scriptural parallels in which this term is used. Romans 6:6, Ephesians 4:22, and Colossians 3:9 all stress the need to put off "the old man" (one's former, sinful self) in order to become a part of the kingdom of heaven.

It is a puzzled Parker who turns and looks behind himself "as if he had expected someone behind him to give him the answer." O'Connor presents the descent of grace on Parker through the use of color and light imagery. As he looks to the east, the sky lightens, and he sees "two or three streaks of yellow (the color of the sun and of di-

vinity) floating above the horizon." He then sees a "tree of light burst
over the horizon." This image, of course, recalls the tree of fire image
which has set him on his final quest. The effect of these events is
to cause him to fall back against the door "as if he had been pinned
there by a lance." With this image, O'Connor ties together the crucifix-
ion ("One of the soldiers opened his side with a lance," John 19:34)
and the earlier passage from Romans 6:6: "For we know that our old
self has been crucified with him, in order that the body of sin may
be destroyed, that we may no longer be slaves to sin."

Now touched by grace, Parker whispers his name through the
keyhole, "and all at once he felt the light pouring through him, turning
his spider web soul into a perfect arabesque of colors, a garden of
trees and birds and beasts." No longer "old O. E." – Parker proclaims
his full name: Obadiah (serving Jah, or God) Elihue (God of him)
unknowingly proclaims his complete acceptance of the Deity. This,
of course, marks the culmination of Parker's desire to emulate the
tattooed man at the fair and brings him to the "destination" toward
which he has been directed since he was fourteen.

When Obadiah Elihue shows his wife the new tattoo, convinced
that "she can't say she don't like the looks of God," her reaction is not
at all what he expects. Steeped in a legalistic-fundamentalist tradition
which looks upon any representation of the Deity as idolatrous, she
declares, "I can put up with lies and vanity but I don't want no idolator
in this house." She then takes up her broom and drives him from the
room, beating him across the shoulders until "large welts had formed
on the face of the tattooed Christ." In the final image of the story,
we see Parker "who called himself Obadiah Elihue – leaning against
the tree, crying like a baby."

The conclusion of the story, while presenting a generally humorous picture, carries with it an expository burden which should not
be overlooked. Obadiah Elihue's suffering clearly places him in the
ranks of the saved as the following passage from the Beatitudes would
indicate: "Blessed are you when men reproach you and persecute you,
and speaking falsely, say all manner of evil against you, for my sake.
Rejoice and exult, because your reward is great in heaven; for so did
they persecute the prophets who were before you" (Matthew 5:11–12).

JUDGEMENT DAY

In her final story, "Judgement Day," O'Connor returned for part of her material to her earliest published story, "The Geranium," which first appeared in 1946. Manuscript evidence indicates that O'Connor reworked the material and entitled it "An Exile in the East" before she finally settled on the present version and title. Both the first and final versions of the story have a displaced Georgian (each of whom has been brought to New York by his daughter) as the protagonist. Both protagonists find the city intolerable and spend a considerable amount of time reminiscing about their old life with a particular Negro companion whom they had grown close to, and both long to return home. For old Dudley, the protagonist of "The Geranium," there is little explicit hope. His story ends with his observation of the geranium, which had, as he observed it in a neighbor's window, become a kind of symbol of his life. Now, the geranium lies smashed in an alley, six floors below his daughter's apartment.

The action of "Judgement Day" covers the final hours of Tanner's life, with flashbacks being utilized to provide additional information about the old man. The story appears to lack the precision of detail which is present in most of O'Connor's other stories, but this minor flaw is probably due to the fact that there was little opportunity for O'Connor to polish the story before her death. It is, however, sufficiently well constructed to convey the author's intent.

Briefly told, the story opens with old Tanner; he is suffering from a stroke which was caused by an earlier encounter with a sour-tempered northern Negro. Tanner is now plotting to escape the city and return home, and he made this decision because two days earlier he heard his daughter and son-in-law decide to ignore their promise to return him to Corinth, Georgia, for burial. As he waits for his daughter to leave the house, his mind wanders back over scenes from his past life. When she leaves the apartment, Tanner makes his way out of the apartment, and he succeeds in getting to the stairs before a second stroke paralyzes his legs and causes him to tumble down the first flight of steps to the landing below.

Tanner is found by the same Negro who slugged him earlier. He asks this Negro, whom he mistakes for his old black friend, Coleman, to help him up, but, instead, the Negro stuffs Tanner's head and legs between the spokes of the banister and leaves him there, where he is found dead by his daughter, when she returns home. The final paragraph of the story details his daughter's decision to have the old man's body dug up and shipped to Georgia, after which she is again able to sleep nights.

Any understanding of this story must be based not upon the sketchy outline presented above, but on the flashbacks which constitute the bulk of the story. After Tanner overhears his daughter and her husband decide to break their promise to return him to Georgia for burial, he chastises her for planning to break her promise, and he lays a curse upon her: "Bury me here and burn in hell!" As she attempts to reason with him and to respond to his curse ("And don't throw hell at me. I don't believe in it. That's a lot of hardshell Baptist hooey"), Tanner's thoughts drift back over the events which brought him to New York.

His daughter found him living in a shack, on land he did not own, with Coleman Parrum, a Negro companion of thirty years. Tanner had become friends with Coleman because of an experience they had years earlier. At that time, Tanner had prided himself particularly on his ability to handle Negro workmen by threatening them with a sharp penknife. When he first saw Coleman, however, he realized that his usual technique would not work. Instead of threatening Coleman, he handed him a pair of wooden glasses, which he had absent-mindedly whittled, and he asked the Negro to put them on. Coleman did so, and when he looked at Tanner and grinned, Tanner had "an instant's sensation of seeing before him a negative image of himself as if clownishness and captivity had been their common lot. The vision failed him before he could decipher it." The result of this epiphanal moment was the establishment of a relationship with Coleman which came to be based on mutual respect and admiration, even though the two men preserved the "appearance" of having established the traditional black-white relationship between them.

Consequently, Tanner comes to the defense of Coleman when Tanner's daughter suggests that duty demands that he move out of the shack that he is sharing with the black man. He tells his daughter that the shack they live in was built by "him and me." He refuses to return to New York with her.

Tanner's plan to stay in Georgia is shattered, however, when a half-breed entrepreneur, Dr. Foley, confronts him on the afternoon of the same day that Tanner has the confrontation with his daughter.

Dr. Foley has purchased the land upon which Tanner and Coleman are squatting, and he informs Tanner that he can stay on the land only if he will operate a still for him. Indignant, Tanner refuses to accept those conditions, and he goes to live in New York with his daughter.

The misery of living in the city destroys at least part of Tanner's pride, for he has decided to return "to squat on the doctor's land and to take orders from a nigger who chewed ten-cent cigars. And to think less about it than formerly."

Tanner's last vestiges of pride are destroyed when he fails to deal properly with a Negro who moves into the apartment house in which Tanner's daughter lives. Motivated, at least partly, by a desire to speak to someone from the South, Tanner thinks to himself, "The nigger would like to talk to someone who understood him." He fails, however, on his first attempt to communicate with the Negro.

For the remainder of the day, Tanner "sat in his chair and debated whether he would have one more try at making friends with him." His further attempt to make friends with the Negro, albeit a somewhat falsely motivated one, sets Tanner somewhat above his daughter, whose plan for getting on with people is to "keep away from them." That afternoon, Tanner makes his second attempt to befriend the black man – only to be told, "I don't take no crap . . . off no wool-hat, red-neck, son-of-a-bitch, peckerwood old bastard like you." When Tanner attempts to pursue the matter further, the Negro knocks him through the door of his daughter's apartment, where he falls "reeling into the living-room."

The stroke which results from that encounter destroys Tanner's plan to leave when his government check comes. When he is able to talk again, he learns that his daughter has used the check for his doctor bills. Denied the option of going to Georgia, Tanner gets his daughter to promise that she will return his corpse to Georgia in a refrigerated car so that he will "keep" on the trip. He then rests peacefully, dreaming of his arrival at the station, where he envisions a red-eyed Coleman and Hooten, the station master, waiting for him. In his dream, he imagines that he springs from the coffin and shouts at the two men, "Judgement Day! Judgement Day! . . . Don't you two fools know it's Judgement Day?"

After he hears his daughter's plan to bury him in New York, Tanner begins to plan his escape. He writes a note directing anyone who finds him dead to ship his body express and collect to Coleman, and then he waits for his opportunity to leave the city, which he describes to Coleman in a letter as "NO KIND OF PLACE." When his daughter leaves the apartment to go to the store, Tanner begins his trip home.

Crippled by the stroke he has had, Tanner finds himself barely able to move. When he stands up, "his body felt like a great heavy bell whose clapper swung from side to side but made no noise." Terrified from fear that he will not be able to make it, he hesitates for a moment. When he finds that he can move without falling over, his confidence returns and he moves – mumbling lines from the 23rd Psalm – toward the sofa, "where he would have support." Although O'Connor uses only the first lines from the 23rd Psalm in the story, the content of the entire psalm is implied, including its conclusion: "and I shall dwell in the house of the Lord for years to come." The reader can assume that O'Connor sees Tanner dwelling "in the house of the Lord for years to come."

Laboriously, Tanner makes his way into the hall and starts for the stairs only to be struck down by another stroke – which causes him to fall down the steps to the first landing. As he lies on the landing, the vision which came to him in his dream appears to him again, and as he regains consciousness, he cries out to the black form leaning over him, "Judgement Day! Judgement Day! You idiots didn't know it was Judgement Day, did you?" For a moment, he becomes rational enough to recognize that the Negro bending over him is not Coleman, that it is the black actor whom Tanner tried earlier to befriend. His final words, "Hep me up, Preacher. I'm on my way home," anger the black man, and he leaves Tanner stuffed through the spokes of the stair bannister to be found by Tanner's daughter.

Tanner's daughter first buries him in New York; but, because she is troubled by guilt, she finally has his remains sent home to Georgia. Tanner's resurrection appears to be anagogically indicated within the story. His dream of being shipped home in his coffin to Corinth, his final words, and the implied final line from the 23rd Psalm make it appear that O'Connor saw Tanner as one of the elect. Thus, Tanner joins the other two characters in O'Connor's final trilogy who are apparently given assurance that their salvation has occurred.

SOME CONCLUDING CONSIDERATIONS

Any individual who works with the fiction of Flannery O'Connor for any length of time cannot help but be impressed by the high degree of mastery she displays in her production of what must ultimately be considered a type of religious propaganda. In story after story, she brings her characters to a moment when it is no longer possible for them to continue in their accustomed manner. The proud are repeatedly humbled, the ignorant are repeatedly enlightened, the wise are repeatedly shown that "the wisdom of this world is foolishness with God," and the materialists are repeatedly forced to recognize that the treasures of this world are theirs to possess for a short time only. Most frequently, as we have seen in the stories, the characters gain their new awareness as a result of having undergone an epiphanal experience.

In many of the stories, the epiphanal moment is accompanied by violence and destruction. In ten of the nineteen stories which appear in her two short story collections, the death of one or more of the characters is used to produce the epiphany. This reinforces O'Connor's comment, "I'm a born Catholic and death has always been a brother to my imagination. I can't imagine a story that doesn't properly end in it or in its foreshadowings." In the remaining stories, the character's epiphany is produced by the destruction of a beloved possession or by the rending of an intellectual veil which has protected the character from the knowledge of his true ignorance.

In none of the stories, however, is the violence used as anything but a logical extension of the action of the story. Never is it used for its own sake. Even more noteworthy, perhaps, is the degree of restraint which O'Connor uses in presenting scenes of violence which, in the hands of a lesser writer, could have been capitalized on for mere shock effect.

For example, the death of the grandmother in "A Good Man Is Hard to Find" is handled in a short statement: ". . . and [he] shot her three times through the chest." The emphasis is immediately shifted then to the effect of the shooting, which is emblematically used to portray her probable salvation. This same tendency to underplay the violence and to accentuate the positive result of the violence on the character is illustrated in the goring to death of Mrs. May in the story "Greenleaf." The charging bull "buried his head in her lap, like a wild tormented lover, before her expression had changed," and she is left at the end of the story appearing "to be bent over whispering some last discovery into the animal's ear." This tendency to rely upon the intellectual rather than on the emotional involvement of the reader in the character's epiphanal moment is characteristic of O'Connor's fiction in general.

O'Connor's tendency to repeat her basic themes with variations from story to story eliminates the possibility that anyone who is familiar with a number of her works is apt to misread them, even though she frequently relies on a rather personal system of symbolism and color imagery to conceal them from the casual reader. That she does so is not unusual, given her view of literature. In "The Nature and Aim of Fiction," she argues "that for the fiction writer himself, symbols are something he uses as a matter of course." She goes on to argue that they have an essential place in the literal level of the story but that they also lead the reader to greater depths of meaning: "The fact that these meanings are there makes the book significant. The reader may not see them but they have their effect on him nonetheless. This is the way the modern novelist sinks, or hides, his theme."

O'Connor's tendency to conceal or "sink" her major themes may, in part, be explained by the attitude which she takes toward her audience. It is this same attitude which may well explain her tendency to deal with grotesque figures. In "The Fiction Writer & His Country," she comments, "The novelist with Christian concerns will find in modern life distortions which are repugnant to him, and his problem will be to make these distortions appear as distortions to an audience which is used to seeing them as natural." She also suggests that an audience which holds views in harmony with those of the author will not need to be violently awakened, but if the audience does not hold similar views, "you have to make your vision apparent by shock—to the hard of hearing you shout, and for the almost blind you draw large and startling figures."

Those readers and critics who see the grotesqueness of a Shiftlet but fail to see in that character a tendency common to all who would bilk the widowed and betray the innocent for the attainment of their own materialistic ends, or look with amazement at a Manley Pointer and choose to ignore all those who likewise pretend to beliefs and lifestyles that are not their own in order that they may pursue their own particular fetishes, provide ample evidence to justify O'Connor's opinion that modern man has generally lost the ability to recognize the perversions which are so much a part of modern society. Thus, when faced with a reminder of his condition, he finds it intolerable. As she notes, "it is only in these centuries when we are afflicted with the doctrine of the perfectibility of human nature by its own efforts that the freak in fiction is so disturbing." This is the case, she argues, "because he keeps us from forgetting that we share in his state. The only time he should be disturbing to us is when he is held up as a whole man." She goes on to comment, "That this happens frequently, I cannot deny, but . . . it indicates a disease, not simply in the novelist but in the society that has given him his values."

O'Connor's concern with the creation of a Christian fiction leads her to recognize that her basic problem will be "trying to get the Christian vision across to an audience to whom it is meaningless." She is aware, however, that she cannot write for a select few. Her insistence that a work of literature must have "value on the dramatic level, the level of truth recognizable by anybody," has made it possible for her to produce a body of literature which contains some stories capable of standing with the best literature written during her era.

In her best stories, then, O'Connor's characters are presented with such fidelity that they become – even when they act in the most outrageous of manners – thoroughly believable. Their actions are those which one would expect from them. Part of her success must be attributed to her ability to select those details and environments which are appropriate to each character. Part, at least, must be attributed to her fine ear for natural dialogue and to her ability to sketch a character with a few deft strokes. In the majority of her stories, the reader is left with the impression that each character – even if one omits the religious aspect of the story – receives exactly what he deserves. The inclusion of the dogma involved provides, as she herself argues, an added dimension to the stories. Thus, O'Connor's greatest achievement as a writer is her ability to arrive at a blend of the religious and the secular in her stories without making apparent, too frequently, the creaking of the machinery from which the God descends.

SUGGESTED ESSAY QUESTIONS

1. Using specific examples from "A Good Man Is Hard to Find," discuss O'Connor's view of the family as she presents it in the story.

2. How are the values of the two main characters in "The Life You Save May Be Your Own" shown to be damaging to the persons who hold them?

3. What are the reasons for and the implications of Harry Ashfield's drowning in "The River"?

4. In what ways does O'Connor use the concept of history in "A Late Encounter with the Enemy"?

5. Discuss the effects of the fear of foreigners (xenophobia) as it influences the actions of the characters in "The Displaced Person."

6. Discuss the initiation motif in "The Artificial Nigger." Do both characters undergo an initiation of sorts?

7. How are the implications of a "belief in nothing" handled in "Good Country People"?

8. Compare and contrast the characters of Julian in "Everything That Rises Must Converge" and Hulga in "Good Country People."

9. What is the significance of the title of "Everything That Rises Must Converge"?

10. In "Revelation," Ruby Turpin experiences a religious vision. How believable is this event as it is presented in the story?

11. Discuss O'Connor's use of the tattoo as a major symbol in "Parker's Back."

12. What does "Judgement Day" have to say about the proper relationships which should be developed between people?

SELECTED BIBLIOGRAPHY

ASALS, FREDERICK. *Flannery O'Connor: The Imagination of Extremity.* Athens, Georgia: The University of Georgia Press, 1982.

BROWNING, PRESTON M., JR. *Flannery O'Connor.* Carbondale: Southern Illinois Press, 1974.

DRAKE, ROBERT. *Flannery O'Connor: A Critical Essay.* Grand Rapids: William B. Erdsmans, 1966.

DRISKELL, LEON V. and JOAN T. BRITTAIN. *The Eternal Crossroads: The Art of Flannery O'Connor.* Lexington: The University Press of Kentucky, 1971.

FEELEY, KATHLEEN. *Flannery O'Connor: Voice of the Peacock.* New Brunswick, New Jersey: Rutgers University Press, 1972.

The Flannery O'Connor Bulletin. Milledgeville, Georgia: Georgia College. Published annually from 1971 to the present.

FRIEDMAN, MELVIN J. and LEWIS A. LAWSON, eds. *The Added Dimension: The Art and Mind of Flannery O'Connor.* New York: Fordham University Press, 1966.

HAWKINS, PETER S. *The Language of Grace: Flannery O'Connor, Walker Percy, and Iris Murdock.* Cambridge, Massachusetts: Cowley Publications, 1983.

HENDIN, JOSEPHINE. *The World of Flannery O'Connor.* Bloomington: Indiana University Press, 1970.

HYMAN, STANLEY EDGAR. *Flannery O'Connor.* University of Minnesota pamphlet No. 54. Minneapolis: University of Minnesota Press, 1966.

MARTIN, CARTER W. *The True Country: Themes in the Fiction of Flannery O'Connor.* Nashville: Vanderbilt University Press, 1969.

MAY, JOHN R. *The Pruning Word: The Parables of Flannery O'Connor.* Notre Dame: University of Notre Dame Press, 1976.

MONTGOMERY, MARION. *Why Flannery O'Connor Stayed Home.* LaSalle: Sherwood Sugden and Company, 1981.

MULLER, GILBERT H. *Nightmares and Visions: Flannery O'Connor and the Catholic Grotesque.* Athens: University of Georgia Press, 1972.

O'CONNOR, FLANNERY. *The Complete Stories.* Ed. Robert Giroux. New York: Farrar, Straus and Giroux, 1971.

_____. *The Habit of Being: Letters of Flannery O'Connor.* Ed. Sally Fitzgerald. New York: Farrar, Straus and Giroux, 1979.

_____. *Mystery and Manners: Occasional Prose.* Ed. Sally Fitzgerald. New York: Farrar, Straus and Cudahay, 1961.

ORVELL, MILES. *Invisible Parade: The Fiction of Flannery O'Connor.* Philadelphia: Temple University Press, 1972.

SCHLOSS, CAROL. *Flannery O'Connor's Dark Comedies: The Limits of Inference.* Baton Rouge: Louisiana State University Press, 1980.

WALTERS, DOROTHY. *Flannery O'Connor. New York: Twayne, 1973.*

NOTES

NOTES